JAMESTOWN  EDUCA'

M000034746

In the Spotlight™

Volume 2

Levels H–J

Henry Billings

Melissa Billings

 **Glencoe**

New York, New York   Columbus, Ohio   Chicago, Illinois   Peoria, Illinois   Woodland Hills, California

JAMESTOWN EDUCATION

ISBN-13: 978-0-07-874325-2
ISBN-10: 0-07-874325-7

Send all queries to:
Glencoe/McGraw-Hill
8787 Orion Place
Columbus, OH 43240-4027

1 2 3 4 5 6 7 8 9 10 021 10 09 08 07 06 05

Contents

To the Student v

How to Use This Book vi

Unit One

1   **Tyra Banks** From "String Bean" to Supermodel 2

2   **Ichiro Suzuki** A Unique Ballplayer 12

3   **Hilary Swank** Learning to Fight 22

Compare and Contrast Chart 32

Unit Two

4   **Ashanti** Holding Her Head High 34

5   **Jon Stewart** Humor with a Bite 44

6   **Chris Klug** A Fortunate and Grateful Athlete 54

Compare and Contrast Chart 64

Unit Three

7   **Antonio Banderas** Making It Big in Hollywood 66

8   **Terrence Howard** The Long Road to Fame 76

9   **Lynne Cox** Extreme Swimmer 86

Compare and Contrast Chart 96

Glossary 97

My Personal Dictionary 101

Writing Checklist 103

Progress Check 104

Comprehension and Critical Thinking Progress Graph 105

Photo Credits 106

To the Student

This book has nine articles about celebrities, or famous people, in the world today. Some of the celebrities are movie or television stars. Some are sports players. Others are authors or musicians.

The lives of these stars can inspire us. Some of the stars had tough times while growing up. They worked very hard to find success. Others had to stay focused on their dreams even when other people thought they would fail. And some had to get through challenges even after they became well-known.

In this book you will work on these three specific reading skills:

Problem and Solution

Making Inferences

Summarizing

You will also work on other reading and vocabulary skills. This will help you understand and think about what you read. The lessons include types of questions often found on state and national tests. Completing the questions can help you get ready for tests you may have to take later.

How to Use This Book

About the Book

This book has three units. Each unit has three lessons. Each lesson has an article about a celebrity followed by practice exercises.

Working Through Each Lesson

Photo Start each lesson by looking at the photo. Read the title and subtitle to get an idea of what the article will focus on.

Think About What You Know, Word Power, Reading Skill This page will help you prepare to read.

Article Now read about the celebrity. Enjoy!

Activities Complete all the activities. Then check your work. Your teacher will give you an answer key to do this. Record the number of your correct answers for each activity. At the end of the lesson, add up your total score for parts A, B, and C. Then find your percentage score in the table. Record your percentage score on the Comprehension and Critical Thinking Progress Graph on page 105.

Compare and Contrast Chart At the end of each unit, you will complete a Compare and Contrast Chart. The chart will help you see what some of the celebrities in the unit have in common.

My Personal Dictionary In the back of this book, you can jot down words you would like to know more about. Later you can ask your teacher or a classmate what the words mean. Then you can add the definitions in your own words.

Tyra Banks

Ichiro Suzuki

Hilary Swank

Tyra Banks

From "String Bean" to Supermodel

Birth Name Tyra Lynne Banks

Birth Date and Place December 4, 1973; Los Angeles, California

Home Los Angeles, California

Think About What You Know

Has anyone ever made fun of you because of how you look? How did that feel? Read the article to find out how Tyra Banks learned to ignore teasing and name-calling and gained self-esteem.

Word Power

What do the words below tell you about the article?

ridicule to laugh at someone or say things to make someone feel foolish

compensate to do something that balances out the effect of a weakness or a loss

alluded talked about something indirectly

rivalries two or more people competing for one thing, especially when they have been competing for a long time

underestimating thinking that someone is not as good or talented as they really are

Reading Skill

Problem and Solution Authors often describe **problems** and **solutions** in their writing. A problem is a situation that causes difficulties. A solution is a way to solve the problem. Taking note of the problems and solutions as you read can help improve your overall understanding of the text.

Example

I love to read. I read books whenever I can. My mother used to worry, saying that I was spending too much time alone. She thought I needed to make more friends. So I joined a book club. I met people who like to read as much as I do. I made a lot of friends through the book club. My mother doesn't worry anymore.

The paragraph shows an example of a problem and a solution. The problem was that *the mother was worried about her daughter spending too much time alone.* What was the solution? How does this solution solve the problem?

Tyra Banks
From "String Bean" to Supermodel

Today Tyra Banks is often called one of the most beautiful women in the world, but as a child the other kids called her less flattering things, such as "Olive Oyl" (the name of the tall, thin girl in the *Popeye* cartoon) and "String Bean." Banks recalls being "super skinny," and it didn't help matters any when she hit a tremendous growth spurt at age 11, losing nearly 30 pounds and gaining four inches in the space of just three months. Even her mother became concerned, taking Banks to doctors to confirm there was nothing medically wrong with her.

2   Banks was so much taller and thinner than her peers that she felt terribly awkward around them. She took refuge in books, spending hours in bookstores near her Los Angeles home and becoming, by her own definition, a "bookworm." This didn't alter her height, but it did help her cope with her unhappiness, transporting her to worlds beyond her immediate surroundings. In high school, she also started working out to build up muscles and add power to her tall frame.

3   As Banks matured, her looks changed. Although she grew to be exceptionally tall—published reports put her anywhere from 5 feet 9 inches to 5 feet 11 inches—she also developed a great complexion and a strikingly attractive face. Still, Banks had learned the hard way that beauty is in the eye of the beholder.

4   It wasn't just her height that caused peers to **ridicule** her. When she was young she was often teased about her high forehead, with people telling her it was so big it could be a "five-head." She says, "In the Black community, a big forehead is a negative thing. You hear that your whole life, but when you go into modeling, it's a positive thing." In fact, Banks says, "When I was a model, it was the one thing that made me more exotic-looking, more interesting. I've always been told

by the fashion industry that if my forehead was an inch smaller, I would have been a little too plain-looking, too pretty-girl-next-door-looking for them. The high forehead set me apart."

5   Before she became a model, Banks often felt humiliated by the teasing she endured, and as a young teenager she desperately wished she could change her physical features to fit society's definition of beauty. In time, though, she realized that the most important thing was not how she appeared to others, but how she felt about herself. She learned to take pride in who she was, not how she looked. As she says, "Self-love has very little to do with how you feel about your outer self. It's about accepting all of yourself."

6   By the time Banks was 17, she was confident enough to imagine herself as a model. She approached several agencies but was turned down by all of them, some saying they didn't need any more African American models and some informing her that she looked "too ethnic." Finally an agency called Elite Model Management Corporation agreed to represent her. Banks wasn't convinced that she would get assignments from them, though, so after high school she made plans to attend college. In August of 1991, just before college started, she was approached by a French modeling agent who happened to be in Los Angeles scouting for new talent. The agent asked Banks to come to Paris and model at an upcoming fashion show.

Skill Break

Problem and Solution

Look at paragraph 5 on this page. This paragraph describes a problem and a solution. The problem was that Banks often felt humiliated when people teased her. What was the **solution?**

How did this **solve the problem?**

7   Banks was thrilled by the opportunity but worried that she wasn't adequately prepared. To **compensate** for her inexperience, she borrowed videotapes from the Fashion Design Institute library and watched fashion and style programs on cable television. Banks then turned her family's living room into a makeshift runway and practiced walking back and forth in her mother's highest heels and longest billowy nightgowns. At first, she says, "my ankles would shake," but with practice she developed a style of movement that was both appealing and distinctive.

8   These self-designed training sessions apparently worked, for when Banks arrived in Paris she became an immediate sensation. At her first modeling show, just two weeks into her Paris stay, Banks sauntered down the runway with such grace that designers scurried to sign her for additional appearances. By the end of the show, she had been offered work in a total of 25 upcoming shows and was being suggested as a cover girl for various European magazines.

9   Entering the world of modeling wasn't completely stress-free for Banks, however. Rumors spread that Naomi Campbell, the other Black supermodel represented by Elite Model, resented Banks and was using her influence in the industry to keep Banks out of certain shows.

10   Banks said little about the conflict at the time, although she later **alluded** to some difficulty by saying, "No model should have to endure what I went through at 17." In any case, Banks remained outwardly calm and dignified and resolved the issue with Campbell by switching to a different modeling agency. A few years later, Banks reflected on the competition among Black models, pointing out that

Fun **F**acts

- Banks does not smoke or drink alcohol.
- She is a big fan of the Los Angeles Lakers basketball team.
- Her personal wealth is estimated at over $8 million.
- She was the first Black model to appear on the covers of the *Sports Illustrated* swimsuit edition and *GQ*.

Tyra Banks gets ready for the camera.

such **rivalries** can be especially fierce because "the fashion business and press can't accept that there can be more than one reigning Black supermodel at a time."

11   Banks spent years working for the biggest names in the fashion industry, but she had other ambitions as well. She pursued acting opportunities, created her own music video, launched her own reality television show, and began hosting her own television talk show. Many people scoffed at these endeavors, **underestimating** her abilities and assuming she was just a "pretty face" without talent. Banks did not allow the criticism to stop her. She had learned to believe in herself, and by working hard she was able to succeed at almost everything she tried. When one of her endeavors failed—such as her attempt to establish herself as a singer—she simply laughed it off and moved on.

12   One of her biggest commitments is to a unique summer camp Banks runs in the mountains outside Los Angeles. Called *Tzone,* it is designed to build self-esteem in teenage girls, encouraging them to explore issues of body image, peer pressure, and self-worth. Banks knows from experience how hard it is for teenage girls to achieve and maintain a positive self-image, and she is determined to help. She wants every young girl to feel beautiful, both inside and out.

A Understanding What You Read

◆ Fill in the circle next to the correct answer.

1. Which of the following statements is an opinion rather than a fact?

○ A. Banks hit a growth spurt at age 11 and lost 30 pounds.

○ B. Banks was taller and thinner than most of her peers.

○ C. Banks is one of the most beautiful women in the world.

2. Banks believes that her high forehead

○ A. has helped her modeling career.

○ B. is much too big for her face.

○ C. makes her look too ethnic.

3. What was the effect of Banks appearing in her first modeling show in Paris?

○ A. Banks was given her own television talk show.

○ B. Banks was sent to a different modeling agency.

○ C. Banks was offered work in 25 other shows.

4. From what you read in the article, which of these is probably true?

○ A. Supermodels get paid very little for their work.

○ B. The modeling industry can be very competitive.

○ C. Most supermodels come from Paris, France.

5. *Tzone* is a summer camp where girls

○ A. learn how to become fashion models.

○ B. try out for a role on a reality show.

○ C. work on developing a positive self-image.

_____ Number of Correct Answers: Part A

B Understanding Problem and Solution

◆ Read the paragraph below. This paragraph describes a problem and a solution. Fill in the circle next to the sentence that **best** describes the **problem.**

1.

Banks was thrilled by the opportunity but worried that she wasn't adequately prepared. To compensate for her inexperience, she borrowed videotapes from the Fashion Design Institute library and watched fashion and style programs on cable television. Banks then turned her family's living room into a makeshift runway and practiced walking back and forth in her mother's highest heels and longest billowy nightgowns. At first, she says, "my ankles would shake," but with practice she developed a style of movement that was both appealing and distinctive.

○ A. Banks was worried that she wasn't adequately prepared.
○ B. Banks watched fashion and style programs on television.
○ C. Banks turned her living room into a makeshift runway.

◆ Reread the paragraph above. What is the **solution** to the problem? How did this solve the problem? Write the solution and how it solved the problem on the lines.

2. Solution: _____

_____

How It Solved the Problem: _____

_____

_____ Number of Correct Answers: Part B

C Using Words

◆ The words and phrases in the list below relate to the words in the box. Some words or phrases in the list have a meaning that is the same as or similar to a word in the box. Some have the opposite meaning. Write the related word from the box on each line. Use each word from the box twice.

ridicule	alluded	underestimating
compensate	rivalries	

Same or similar meaning

1. competitions _____

2. making less _____

3. make up for _____

4. criticize _____

5. balance _____

6. hinted _____

Opposite meaning

7. praise _____

8. exaggerating _____

9. stated clearly _____

10. partnerships _____

_____ Number of Correct Answers: Part C

D Writing About It

Write a Journal Entry

◆ Suppose you had attended the 1991 Paris fashion show where Banks made her debut. Write a journal entry about what you saw that day. Be sure to describe the way Banks looked and her modeling style. Write **at least four** sentences. Use the checklist on page 103 to check your work.

_____

_____

_____

_____

_____

_____

_____

_____

Lesson 1 Add your correct answers from parts A, B, and C to get your total score. Then find the percentage for your total score on the chart below. Record your percentage on the graph on page 105.

_____ Total Score for Parts A, B, and C

_____ Percentage

Total Score	1	2	3	4	5	6	7	8	9	10	11	12	13	14	15	16	17
Percentage	6	12	18	24	29	35	41	47	53	59	65	70	76	82	88	94	100

Ichiro Suzuki

A Unique Ballplayer

Birth Name Ichiro Suzuki

Birth Date and Place October 22, 1973; Kasugai, Japan

Home Seattle, Washington

Think About What You Know

Do you know people who have their own unique style? What makes their style unique? Read the article to find out about Ichiro Suzuki's baseball talent and his unique style.

Word Power

What do the words below tell you about the article?

surname the name that a person shares with his or her family; in English it is the person's last name

aptitude a natural skill or ability to learn

individuality the qualities that make a person different from others

conformity behavior that follows the same rules or ideas that are accepted by most other people in society

charisma the ability to easily attract other people and get them to like you

Reading Skill

Make Inferences Authors don't always say everything they want the reader to understand. Sometimes authors hint at what they mean by providing clues. Good readers **make inferences.** To make an inference, use the author's clues and your own knowledge or experiences to fill in information about the people, places, and events described in the text.

Example

Professional baseball is a very popular sport in Japan. Founded in 1936, *Pro Yakyu* consists of two baseball leagues, each with six teams. Most of the *Pro Yakyu* games are broadcast live on television.

This example contains a hint about how Japanese baseball compares with American baseball. Using this hint and what you already know, you can infer that *Japanese baseball is similar to American baseball.* How does what you already know support this inference?

Ichiro Suzuki

A Unique Ballplayer

When baseball superstar Ichiro Suzuki left Japan to play for the Seattle Mariners in November 2000, he made one special request. Although all other major league baseball players have their **surname** embroidered on the back of their uniform for easy identification by fans, Ichiro wanted his jersey to say *Ichiro,* not *Suzuki.* Ichiro was what everyone in Japan called him, and it was how he wanted to be known in the United States as well. Given his incredible fame in his home country, U.S. baseball officials granted this unusual request.

2 Ichiro's celebrity status was established in Japan in the 1990s when he played outfield for nine seasons in his country's version of major league baseball. During that time he won seven consecutive batting titles and seven Gold Gloves for his defensive play. Along the way, he became one of the most adored athletes in Japanese history.

3 Part of what made Ichiro so appealing was his skill as a player. Since he'd first stepped onto a baseball diamond at age six, he had shown not only amazing **aptitude** for the game but also tremendous discipline in developing his talents. When he was seven, he and his father had devised a daily training schedule that called for Ichiro to throw 50 pitches, field 50 infield balls and 50 outfield balls, and hit at least 450 pitches. So by the time Ichiro turned pro, his skills were razor sharp.

4 There was another factor that elevated Ichiro above ordinary stardom, and that was his extreme **individuality.** Historically the Japanese have valued **conformity,** but Ichiro grew up at a time when the younger generation was beginning to value personal self-expression, so his unique style became a symbol of individual freedom. In contrast to his somber teammates, Ichiro sported spiky hair and wraparound sunglasses. He showed equal flair on the field,

where he took an offbeat approach to everything from running the bases to doing warm-up exercises. At the plate, he pointed his bat at the pitcher as if it was a sword, and when he swung the bat he used an exaggerated leg kick to generate additional power. "It was part of my image," explains Ichiro, who added, "if you think Ichiro, you think of the leg kick."

5   There was simply no other Japanese player like him. Ted Heid, the Seattle Mariners' director in Asia, was impressed by Ichiro's **charisma,** saying, "The first time I saw him play in Japan, it was unbelievable. If there were 40,000 people in the stadium, 39,999 of them were cheering for Ichiro." Ichiro was so famous that he claimed a letter addressed simply "Ichiro, Japan" would have no trouble reaching its destination.

6   Such fame did have its dark side. Ichiro's fans gave him no privacy or personal space. "In Japan," Ichiro said, "I can't use a public restroom along the highway," since "for me to stop at a large public restroom would be asking for trouble." He could not leave his apartment without being followed or eat in a restaurant without a group of bodyguards to shield him from other diners. Unable to marry his girlfriend, Yumiko Fukushima, in Japan because of his popularity, he fled to California with her under an assumed name and had the wedding ceremony there.

Skill Break
Make Inferences
Look at paragraph 5 on this page. The paragraph gives hints about Ichiro's popularity.

What can you **infer** about Ichiro's fame in Japan?

What **clue** supports your inference?

How does **what you already know** help you make this inference?

7   Even when he reported to spring training with the Mariners in 2001, Ichiro could not escape a swarm of Japanese reporters. They reported on everything from the practice swings he took in the batting cage to the fly balls he shagged in the outfield to the type of rice balls his wife packed in his lunch. It was even said that one Japanese publisher was offering $2 million for a clubhouse picture of Ichiro in the nude—a rumor that forced Ichiro to begin changing in a private area of the Mariners' locker room.

8   Despite the fascination with Ichiro's daily schedule, the biggest question on everyone's mind was whether or not Ichiro was good enough to become a top ballplayer in the U.S. leagues. A few Japanese players had been successful in the United States, but they were all pitchers. Ichiro, at 5 feet 9 inches and 170 pounds, was very small for an outfielder. How would he fare against the much bigger and stronger American players?

9   It didn't take long for Ichiro to answer that question. He went on two early hitting streaks—one lasted 15 games and the other lasted 23 games—leading the Mariners to victory after victory. By the All-Star game, Seattle fans were suffering from the same "Ichiro Mania" that had afflicted fans in Japan. Hot dogs stands at the Mariners' home stadium even began selling "Ichi Rolls," inspired by a kind of Japanese food called *sushi* made with spicy fish, rice, and vegetables. Meanwhile, back in Japan, enthusiastic fans lined up to pay $2,000 for round-trip packages from Japan to Seattle to see their hero play for the Mariners.

10   The 2001 regular season was a huge success for both the Mariners and Ichiro. The team finished with an extraordinary record of 116 wins and only 46 losses and breezed into the West Division championship of the American League leading by 14 games. They went on to

Fun **F**acts

▶ *Ichiro* means "first son" in Japanese.

▶ Ichiro likes rap music.

▶ Ichiro's favorite food is beef tongue.

▶ He is right-handed, but he learned to bat lefty just so he could stand a couple of steps closer to first base.

Ichiro Suzuki watches his double-base hit fly into left field during a game against the New York Yankees.

eliminate the Cleveland Indians in the first round of the playoffs, thanks in large part to Ichiro's 12 hits and record-setting .600 batting average. Unfortunately, the Mariners stumbled against the talented New York Yankees in the next round, losing four games to one.

11 For his own efforts, Ichiro won just about every award possible. He won a Gold Glove award for making only one error all year and captured the American League batting title. Despite his embarrassment at being considered a rookie, he won the American League Rookie of the Year Award, and he took home the biggest prize of all when he was voted the American League's Most Valuable Player. Clearly he had erased all doubts about his ability to compete against the best U.S. players.

12 Since 2001 Ichiro has continued his brilliant career, setting all kinds of hitting records. He became the first player to collect more than 200 hits in each of his first four years in the major leagues. His greatest achievement came in 2004 when he broke George Sisler's record of 257 hits in a single season. Experts had long thought the record—set in 1920—would never be broken, but Ichiro beat it by five hits.

13 In 2005 opposing pitcher Mark Buehrle was asked what approach he used when facing Ichiro. Buehrle just shrugged and said, "I don't want to analyze Ichiro. What's the point? He hits everything."

A Understanding What You Read

◆ Fill in the circle next to the correct answer or write the answer.

1. Ichiro made an unusual decision when he chose to

   ○ A. play outfield for nine seasons in a row.
   ○ B. wear his first name on his baseball jersey.
   ○ C. practice catching and hitting every day.

2. Ichiro could not have his wedding in Japan because

   ○ A. he was too busy playing for the Mariners.
   ○ B. his girlfriend was living in the United States.
   ○ C. his popularity left him with no privacy.

3. In which paragraph did you find the information to answer question 2?

   _____

4. Which sentence **best** states the main idea of the article?

   ○ A. Ichiro Suzuki is a talented and well-loved baseball hero with a unique style.
   ○ B. Ichiro Suzuki is so popular that he has to work hard to protect his personal life.
   ○ C. Ichiro Suzuki began his career in Japan and then came to the United States.

5. From the information in the article, you can predict that

   ○ A. Ichiro will move back to Japan.
   ○ B. Ichiro will break more records.
   ○ C. Ichiro will be traded to the Yankees.

_____ Number of Correct Answers: Part A

B Making Inferences

◆ Read the paragraph below. Using the author's hints and what you already know, what can you infer about Ichiro's childhood? Fill in the circle next to the inference that is **best** supported by the paragraph. Then underline **one** hint in the paragraph that supports this inference.

1.

   Part of what made Ichiro so appealing was his skill as a player. Since he'd first stepped onto a baseball diamond at age six, he had shown not only amazing aptitude for the game but also tremendous discipline in developing his talents. When he was seven, he and his father had devised a daily training schedule that called for Ichiro to throw 50 pitches, field 50 infield balls and 50 outfield balls, and hit at least 450 pitches. So by the time Ichiro turned pro, his skills were razor sharp.

   ○ A. Ichiro and his father did not get along very well.
   ○ B. Ichiro did not spend a lot of time with his friends.
   ○ C. Ichiro worked hard at school and earned good grades.

◆ Reread paragraph 9 in the article. What inference can you make about how Ichiro's Japanese fans felt after Ichiro moved to Seattle? Write your inference below. Then write the clue you used and explain how what you already know helped you make this inference.

2. Inference: _____

   Clue: _____

   What I Know: _____

   _____

   ┌───┐
   │ _____ Number of Correct Answers: Part B   │
   └───┘

C Using Words

◆ Complete each sentence with a word from the box. Write the
missing word on the line.

surname	individuality	charisma
aptitude	conformity	

1. The beautiful short story she wrote demonstrated her great

   _____ for creative writing.

2. The politician had enough _____ to make the people
   want to elect him.

3. A person with original ideas might feel uncomfortable in a group

   that encourages _____.

4. He expresses his _____ through his unusual
   collection of music.

5. I have a Spanish _____ because my father's family is
   from Mexico.

◆ Choose one of the words from the box. Write a new sentence
using the word.

6. word: _____

   _____

_____

_____ Number of Correct Answers: Part C

D Writing About It

Write a Speech

◆ Suppose Ichiro Suzuki was coming to your school and you have been asked to introduce him to the other students. Write a speech that describes Ichiro's baseball career and the qualities that make him unique. Write **at least four** sentences. Use the checklist on page 103 to check your work.

_____

_____

_____

_____

_____

_____

_____

_____

Lesson 2 Add your correct answers from parts A, B, and C to get your total score. Then find the percentage for your total score on the chart below. Record your percentage on the graph on page 105.

_____ Total Score for Parts A, B, and C

_____ Percentage

Total Score	1	2	3	4	5	6	7	8	9	10	11	12	13
Percentage	8	15	23	31	38	46	54	62	69	77	85	92	100

Hilary Swank

Learning to Fight

Birth Name Hilary Ann Swank

Birth Date and Place July 30, 1974; Lincoln, Nebraska

Homes New York City and Los Angeles, California

Think About What You Know

Have you ever watched a boxing match? Did you like it? Read the article to find out how Hilary Swank came to respect the sport of boxing.

Word Power

What do the words below tell you about the article?

eluded escaped someone's understanding

nutritionist someone who knows the right foods to eat for good health

assimilate to take in, absorb, and use in the body

diagnosis the process of looking at a person closely to find out what is wrong with them

euphoria a feeling of extreme joy and excitement

Reading Skill

Summarizing A **summary** is a shortened version of a paragraph or article written in your own words. A summary includes only the most important ideas from the text. When you read, look for key words and phrases that give information about *who, what, where, when, how,* or *why*. This information explains the important ideas. The summary of a paragraph should be logical and no more than three sentences long.

Example

When Laila Ali made her debut in professional women's boxing, the media was watching closely. This was because Laila Ali is the daughter of legendary boxer Muhammad Ali. When she won her first match in only 31 seconds, skeptics said the match was staged to provide her with an easy win. However, Laila Ali went on to win time and time again, becoming a champion in women's boxing.

Two important ideas in this paragraph are *Laila Ali is the daughter of boxer Muhammad Ali* and *at first people thought her boxing success was staged.* These ideas should be included in a summary of this paragraph. What is the third important idea that should be included? Why is it important?

23

Hilary Swank

Learning to Fight

Before 2004 Hilary Swank didn't know anything about boxing. She had never paid much attention to the sport, and when it did occasionally flit into her consciousness, her reaction was one of puzzlement. As she puts it, "I just thought, 'What is the thing about hitting someone and wanting to get hit? Where's the pleasure in it?' The whole thing **eluded** me."

2   Swank's attitude changed after she agreed to play the lead role in the movie *Million Dollar Baby,* the story of a female boxer determined to establish herself in the boxing ring. In the course of preparing for this movie, Swank not only gained a new appreciation for boxing but also became a pretty decent boxer herself.

3   When Swank was offered the part, she was already an Oscar winner, having earned an Academy Award for Best Actress for her role in *Boys Don't Cry* (1999). Since she hadn't had a hit movie since then, she concluded that great roles simply "don't come around very often." When she read the script for *Million Dollar Baby,* she says, "I couldn't believe how beautiful it was." She knew immediately that she wanted to be part of it.

4   The movie focuses on a 32-year-old restaurant worker named Maggie Fitzgerald, a woman with no money but with a dream of becoming a professional boxer. The impoverished background of the character is one Swank could identify with, for she herself grew up poor, living most of her childhood in a trailer park in Bellingham, Washington. Her parents had a troubled marriage, and as a young girl Swank often felt lonely and neglected. Like Fitzgerald, Swank had a dream, and, like Fitzgerald, she was determined to pursue it.

5   By the time she was 15, Swank's parents had separated and her mother had lost her job. Despite their lack of resources, Swank and

her mother decided to move to Hollywood so Swank could try to turn her acting fantasies into reality.

6　　When they arrived in Hollywood, Swank and her mother had no housing, no jobs, and just $75 in cash. Swank had no résumé or glossy photos to send out to studios. Operating out of their car, they used pay phones to call agents, and, since they had no phone number where they could be called back, their only hope was to set up a face-to-face meeting while they had the agent on the phone. Fortunately, an agent named Bonnie Liedtke agreed to meet Swank. Liedtke liked what she saw and promptly signed Swank to a contract.

7　　For several years after that, Swank considered herself fortunate to be employed as an actor in any capacity. She was given roles in *Buffy the Vampire Slayer* (1992) and *The Next Karate Kid* (1994), but it was *Boys Don't Cry* that made her famous. Although she was paid only $75 per day—a total of $3,000 for the entire movie—her performance as Teena Brandon, a girl who pretends to be a boy, established her as an actor of distinction.

8　　With *Million Dollar Baby,* Swank saw another opportunity to make a top-notch film—and also to challenge herself as an actor. To play Fitzgerald, she would need to immerse herself in training so that she could be convincing in fight scenes. With only three months until filming was slated to begin, Swank had no time to lose. She went to work with a weight trainer, a boxing trainer, and a **nutritionist,** trying to strengthen her body and gain 10 pounds of muscle while learning the hand, foot, and body movements of a fighter.

Skill Break

Summarizing

Look at paragraph 8 on this page. This paragraph describes what Swank needed to do to prepare for her role in *Million Dollar Baby*.

What **key words** help you find the **most important ideas** in the paragraph?

What are the **three most important ideas** in the paragraph?

9   Swank describes her training schedule this way: "I lived, slept, ate, breathed, and drank boxing." She worked out for at least four hours a day, six days a week. While U.S. dietary guidelines recommend that an average woman take in about 50 grams of protein daily, Swank was consuming more than four times that much, gulping down egg whites and raw fish. As she says, "Eating 210 grams of protein a day meant I had to eat every hour and a half" because a person's body "can only **assimilate** so much protein at a time." Therefore, although she needed nine hours of sleep each night to recover from her daytime training sessions, she had to wake up in the night to guzzle a protein shake.

10   As the weeks passed, Swank put on pound after pound of pure muscle, and, as her boxing trainer said, she "gained the confidence she needed, and started boxing like a real boxer." There were plenty of rough patches along the way. She admits "waking up some days and saying: 'I can't. My body hurts, I'm exhausted, I've already worked out 20 hours this week.'" Still, she pushed herself to keep going, driving herself so hard that she almost ran into serious problems.

11   Swank developed a painful blister on her foot, but she ignored it. She kept training and didn't seek medical attention—until the day she saw bright streaks running through her foot. The doctor told her that the blister had caused a bacterial infection and that if she had waited two more hours she would have required weeks of hospitalization. He also told her that if the infection had spread to her heart, it would have killed her.

Fun Facts

▶ Swank loves pets and has many animals, including a dog, cat, rabbit, and parrot.

▶ When she was young, Swank was a Junior Olympic swimmer.

▶ She says the biggest lesson she has learned is to follow her own heart.

Hilary Swank performs a scene with Clint Eastwood in *Million Dollar Baby.*

12   Swank calmly accepted the **diagnosis,** began taking medication, and then continued her training after only a few days of rest. As she says, "In the end, that's what happens to boxers: they get blisters, they get infected. They have injuries, and they keep pushing through it."

13   By the time filming started, Swank had added 19 pounds to her 5-foot-5-inch frame and was a powerful enough boxer to bring the role of Maggie Fitzgerald to life. Beyond the fight scenes, the role required Swank to display a wide range of emotions, moving from desperation to hope to **euphoria,** then back down to anguish and resignation. Audiences and critics alike praised her performance, and she became the fifth female actor to be nominated twice for an Academy Award and then win both times.

14   Swank was grateful to have had the chance to play the role of Maggie Fitzgerald. She was also grateful for the insights that *Million Dollar Baby* had given her into the world of boxing. "I love boxing now," she told one reporter, "and have an enormous amount of respect for boxers as athletes because boxing is . . . the most physically challenging thing I have ever done."

A Understanding What You Read

◆ Fill in the circle next to the correct answer.

1. The main character in *Million Dollar Baby* is

○ A. an actor named Buffy.

○ B. a girl named Teena Brandon.

○ C. a woman named Maggie Fitzgerald.

2. From what the article told you about Hilary Swank you can conclude that she

○ A. knew a lot about boxing even before *Million Dollar Baby*.

○ B. is willing to do whatever it takes to realize her goals.

○ C. plans to return to her hometown in Washington one day.

3. When Swank first arrived in Hollywood, she had

○ A. only $75 in cash.

○ B. two movie offers.

○ C. a serious leg infection.

4. The author probably wrote this article in order to

○ A. inform the reader about an award-winning actor.

○ B. convince the reader that boxing is a dangerous sport.

○ C. teach the reader how to get started in an acting career.

5. Which of the following categories would this article **best** fit into?

○ A. Greatest Athletes of All Time

○ B. Actors Who Accept Difficult Roles

○ C. Hollywood Movies That Make Us Think

_____ Number of Correct Answers: Part A

B Summarizing

◆ Read the paragraph below. Underline the key words and phrases that explain the most important ideas. Then fill in the circle next to the statement that **best** summarizes the paragraph.

1.

The movie focuses on a 32-year-old restaurant worker named Maggie Fitzgerald, a woman with no money but with a dream of becoming a professional boxer. The impoverished background of the character is one Swank could identify with, for she herself grew up poor, living most of her childhood in a trailer park in Bellingham, Washington. Her parents had a troubled marriage, and as a young girl Swank often felt lonely and neglected. Like Fitzgerald, Swank had a dream, and, like Fitzgerald, she was determined to pursue it.

○ A. Maggie Fitzgerald was 32 years old when she started dreaming of becoming a professional boxer. She worked in a restaurant and had very little money.

○ B. Hilary Swank grew up poor, so she could identify with Maggie Fitzgerald's story. Like Fitzgerald, Swank was determined to follow her dream.

○ C. Hilary Swank grew up in a trailer park in Washington. She often felt lonely and neglected, but she didn't let her troubles get in the way of her dream.

◆ Reread paragraph 11 in the article. Write the **three** most important ideas in the paragraph on the lines. Then, in your own words, write a summary of the paragraph in two or three sentences.

2. Most Important Ideas: _____

Summary:_____

_____ Number of Correct Answers: Part B

C Using Words

◆ Cross out one of the four words in each row that does **not** relate to the word in dark type.

1. eluded

escape   increase   mystery   lost

2. nutritionist

protein   diet   letter   vitamin

3. assimilate

mix   absorb   digest   reverse

4. diagnosis

doctor   recipe   study   illness

5. euphoria

direction   happy   good   emotion

◆ Choose one of the words shown in dark type above. Write a sentence using the word.

6. word: _____

_____

_____

_____ Number of Correct Answers: Part C

D Writing About It

Write a Postcard

◆ Write a postcard to Hilary Swank. Be sure to write about some of the things you learned from the article. Write **at least four** sentences. Use the checklist on page 103 to check your work.

Dear Ms. Swank,

_____

_____

_____

_____

_____

_____

Sincerely,

_____

Ms. Hilary Swank
789 Swank Ln.
Hilaryville, USA

Lesson 3 Add your correct answers from parts A, B, and C to get your total score. Then find the percentage for your total score on the chart below. Record your percentage on the graph on page 105.

_____ Total Score for Parts A, B, and C

_____ Percentage

Total Score	1	2	3	4	5	6	7	8	9	10	11	12	13
Percentage	8	15	23	31	38	46	54	62	69	77	85	92	100

Compare and Contrast

◆ Think about the celebrities in Unit One. Which two articles tell about celebrities who experienced a change in their physical appearance? Use information from the articles to fill in this chart.

Celebrity's Name		
What physical change did the celebrity experience?		
What caused the celebrity's physical appearance to change?		
How did the change affect the celebrity's life?		

Ashanti

Jon Stewart

Chris Klug

Ashanti
Holding Her Head High

Birth Name Ashanti Shequoiya Douglas
Birth Date and Place October 13, 1980; Glen Cove, Long Island, New York
Home Long Island, New York

Think About What You Know

Have you ever had to give up a good thing in order to have something else that you really wanted? Read the article to find out what Ashanti chose to give up in order to pursue her singing career.

Word Power

What do the words below tell you about the article?

persevered kept on trying to do something in a determined way despite difficulties

backlash a strong reaction by a number of people against an event or a decision

perception the ideas that a person has formed about something

composure calmness

adversity a situation that brings a lot of problems or hardships

Reading Skill

Problem and Solution Authors often describe **problems** and **solutions** in their writing. A problem is a situation that causes difficulties. A solution is a way to solve the problem. Taking note of the problems and solutions as you read can help improve your overall understanding of the text.

Example

One of my friends is a top runner on the cross-country team. Last year she won the school award for best athlete. Many students were angry. They didn't think she deserved it. However, when she came in first place at the state championship, people realized how talented she was and the whole school celebrated.

The paragraph shows an example of a problem and a solution. The problem is that *people didn't think the friend deserved the award*. What was the solution? How did this solution solve the problem?

Ashanti

Holding Her Head High

Ashanti Douglas grew up dancing. Her mother, a dance instructor, started her off with lessons at the age of three, and eventually Ashanti was skilled at everything from tap dance and ballet to jazz and hip-hop to traditional African dance. Not only was she an accomplished dancer, but she was athletic in other ways as well, running so fast and jumping so far that she became a track star at her Long Island high school. In addition, she was a strong student and a good writer and even won contests for some of her early compositions. Ashanti had so many talents that although she sang in her church choir, for years no one really noticed her beautiful singing voice.

2   That changed one day when 12-year-old Ashanti was doing some household chores for her mother. As she recalls, "I was downstairs vacuuming and my mom said, 'No television or radio until your chores are done. Turn the radio off!'" Ashanti called back, "Ma, that's not the radio—that's me." Indeed, Ashanti was singing the Mary J. Blige song "Reminisce" and doing such a convincing job that she sounded like the famous R&B recording artist herself. Stunned to discover how beautifully their daughter sang, Ashanti's parents quickly went in search of a record deal for her.

3   At age 14, Ashanti signed a contract with Jive Records, the same company that worked with Britney Spears and the group 'N Sync. "They would send a car to pick me up in high school," Ashanti recalls, adding, "I'd have my books, do my homework, start recording, and they'd have a car to bring me back home." This might have seemed glamorous, but actually Ashanti had a troubled relationship with the company. According to one report, she was unhappy because studio executives wanted to shape her into a pop star and were not interested in letting her write her own songs.

4   Eventually, the recording deal went bad and Ashanti was released from her contract. For some aspiring young singers, this would have been devastating, but Ashanti refused to let it bother her. Instead, she refocused all her attention on her high school life, excelling in her classes and setting triple jump records on her track team.

5   When Ashanti was 17, a different recording company offered her a contract. Sony's Epic Records wanted her, but accepting their deal meant moving to Atlanta, Georgia, and sacrificing a track-and-field scholarship she had won to Hampton University. It was a tough decision, but the promise of stardom was too great to ignore, and ultimately Ashanti turned down the scholarship, gave up college, and headed off to Atlanta.

6   Unfortunately for her, this deal didn't work out any better than the previous one had: her contact at Epic soon lost his job, and the company fired all the performers he had brought in. That meant Ashanti suddenly had no contract, no connections, and no prospects.

7   Disappointed and discouraged, she returned home to New York, where, as she recalls, "All of my friends are coming back from college, and they're talking about classes and new guys and parties and stuff that's going on." The uncertainty about her future singing career was difficult for her to accept, but nonetheless Ashanti **persevered.** She decided to get a job as a telemarketer and as a childcare worker to pay the bills and enrolled in a couple of college courses, but she reserved most of her energy for the pursuit of another recording contract.

Skill Break
Problem and Solution
Look at paragraph 4 on this page. This paragraph describes a problem and a solution. The problem was that Ashanti's recording deal went bad and she was released from her contract. What was the **solution?**

How did this **solve the problem?**

8   In 2000 she succeeded in signing with Murder, Inc., a company that produced many successful rap albums. Executives there paired Ashanti's sweet, tender voice with the voice of several hard-edged rappers, which resulted in some tremendous hit songs that thrust Ashanti into the spotlight. Soon she had three songs in the Top 10, and her 2002 self-titled album also soared to number one, selling a total of six million copies.

9   There was trouble ahead, however. It started with critics grumbling that Ashanti's reputation was inflated and that her commercial success was greater than her talent warranted. While some hailed "the purity of her voice" as "irresistible," others attacked her, questioning how much ability she really had. One reviewer declared that Ashanti's album had "the inspirational appeal of a hospital waiting room."

10   Things got worse when Ashanti was given the Soul Train Aretha Franklin Award for 2002, which outraged music fans. Since the award honors the entertainer of the year, many people didn't believe Ashanti deserved the award as much as performers such as Alicia Keys or Faith Evans. These music buffs started an online petition to protest Ashanti's selection, ultimately gathering more than 30,000 signatures against her.

11   This was a stressful experience for Ashanti, and she remarks, "I almost threw up about the Aretha Franklin Award **backlash.**" She tried hard to understand why she was being attacked, concluding, "The **perception** was that it came too easily for me. It didn't, but it looked that way." She was, in her words, "from the not-so-mean streets of Long Island" and led a comfortable life that didn't involve drinking, smoking, or drugs, so "people think I haven't suffered

Fun Facts

▸ Ashanti is the first performer since the Beatles to have three songs on the Billboard Top Ten at the same time.

▸ She is named after a West African tribe in the country that is now known as Ghana.

enough." All that the public saw was a singer who hadn't "paid her dues." Although it was difficult to be so publicly insulted, Ashanti maintained her **composure,** accepted the award proudly, and then quietly went back to work on her music.

12   The next two years were not easy ones for Ashanti. Her second album sold less than half of what her first one had, and a Christmas album she put out sold a meager 100,000 copies. In addition, there was a lot of negative publicity surrounding her record label's name, Murder, Inc. In 2003 Ashanti and others associated with the recording studio got together and agreed on a name change, so that Murder, Inc. became simply The Inc. That opened up new endorsement possibilities, and Ashanti soon became the spokesperson for a prominent brand of hair care products.

13   Ashanti worked at rebuilding her image in other ways as well. Not only did she put out a new album, titled *Concrete Rose,* in 2004, but she also started an acting career, appearing in the movies *Bride and Prejudice* (2004) and *Coach Carter* (2005). In addition, she launched her own perfume and a special line of jeans. By refusing to be defeated by **adversity** and by continuing to put forth her best effort, Ashanti showed she was not only talented but tough as well.

A Understanding What You Read

◆ Fill in the circle next to the correct answer.

1. From what you read in the article, which of these is probably true?

   ○ A. As a child, Ashanti didn't have to do household chores.
   ○ B. As a child, Ashanti rarely sang when her mother was around.
   ○ C. As a child, Ashanti spent most of her free time studying.

2. What caused Ashanti to give up her college track scholarship?

   ○ A. She decided to move to Atlanta to record her music.
   ○ B. She started to focus all of her energy on a dance career.
   ○ C. She wanted to start working in telemarketing and childcare.

3. Ashanti achieved her first big success after she

   ○ A. appeared in the movie *Coach Carter*.
   ○ B. won the Soul Train Aretha Franklin Award.
   ○ C. signed a recording contract with Murder, Inc.

4. Ashanti believes her critics don't like her because she

   ○ A. was once a track star.
   ○ B. has led a comfortable life.
   ○ C. has not won any awards.

5. Which sentence **best** states the lesson about life that this article teaches?

   ○ A. The best opportunity is the first opportunity.
   ○ B. Determination and inner strength lead to success.
   ○ C. Famous people are rarely criticized for what they do.

_____ Number of Correct Answers: Part A

B Understanding Problem and Solution

◆ Read the paragraphs below. The paragraphs describe a problem and a solution. Fill in the circle next to the sentence that **best** describes the **problem.**

1.

Unfortunately for her, this deal didn't work out any better than the previous one had: her contact at Epic soon lost his job, and the company fired all the performers he had brought in. That meant Ashanti suddenly had no contract, no connections, and no prospects.

Disappointed and discouraged, she returned home to New York, where, as she recalls, "All of my friends are coming back from college, and they're talking about classes and new guys and parties and stuff that's going on." The uncertainty about her future singing career was difficult for her to accept, but nonetheless Ashanti persevered. She decided to get a job as a telemarketer and as a childcare worker to pay the bills and enrolled in a couple of college courses, but she reserved most of her energy for the pursuit of another recording contract.

○ A. Ashanti had no contract, no connections, and no prospects.
○ B. Ashanti's friends were coming back from college and talking about their classes.
○ C. Ashanti reserved her energy for the pursuit of another contract.

◆ Reread the paragraph above. What is the **solution** to the problem? How did this solve the problem? Write the solution and how it solved the problem on the lines.

2. Solution: _____

How It Solved the Problem: _____

_____ Number of Correct Answers: Part B

C Using Words

◆ Complete the analogies below by writing a word from the box on each line. Remember that in an analogy, the last two words or phrases must be related in the same way that the first two are related.

persevered	perception	adversity
backlash	composure	

1. dish : plate :: thought : _____

2. apart : together :: hysteria : _____

3. color : brown :: reaction : _____

4. try : attempt :: continued : _____

5. music : song :: trouble : _____

◆ Choose one word from the box. Write a sentence using the word.

6. word: _____

_____

_____

_____ Number of Correct Answers: Part C

D Writing About It

Write a Magazine Article

◆ Suppose you were a reporter covering the music industry in 2002. Write an article about Ashanti winning the Soul Train Aretha Franklin Award. Write **at least four** sentences. Use the checklist on page 103 to check your work.

_____

_____

_____

_____

_____

_____

_____

_____

Lesson 4 Add your correct answers from parts A, B, and C to get your total score. Then find the percentage for your total score on the chart below. Record your percentage on the graph on page 105.

_____ Total Score for Parts A, B, and C

_____ Percentage

Total Score	1	2	3	4	5	6	7	8	9	10	11	12	13
Percentage	8	15	23	31	38	46	54	62	69	77	85	92	100

Jon Stewart
Humor with a Bite

Birth Name Jonathan Stuart Leibowitz

Birth Date and Place November 28, 1962; New York City

Home New York City

Think About What You Know

Do you have a favorite news show or a favorite comedian? Read the article to find out how Jon Stewart combines news and humor.

Word Power

What do the words below tell you about the article?

parodies imitations of something or someone that are done in a humorous way

relevant directly relating to a current issue or topic of discussion

satire a way of criticizing something or someone using humor, so that their faults can be seen more clearly

wry knowing a situation is bad, but also thinking it is rather funny

deconstruct to analyze something with the belief that there is no single explanation or meaning

Reading Skill

Make Inferences Authors don't always say everything they want the reader to understand. Sometimes authors hint at what they mean by providing clues. Good readers **make inferences.** To make an inference, use the author's clues and your own knowledge or experiences to fill in information about the people, places, and events described in the text.

Example

Comedians like to make us laugh. Some comedians get laughs by being clumsy just when they are trying to impress someone. Others make us laugh by acting like they are smarter than other people, but then saying something silly, such as, "There are three kinds of people; those who can count and those who cannot."

One inference that the reader can make is that *people often think it's funny when something ironic happens.* One clue that supports this inference is "acting like they are smarter . . . but then saying something silly." How does what you already know support this inference?

Jon Stewart

Humor with a Bite

When Jon Stewart took over as host of Comedy Central's *The Daily Show* in 1999, he wanted to make some significant changes. Before Stewart joined the show, this late-night television broadcast had entertained viewers by presenting a "faux," or fake, news show that featured celebrity jokes and **parodies** of ordinary citizens with weird hobbies or ridiculous beliefs.

2   Stewart wanted to address more **relevant** topics, while still using humor. As he says, "It was a conscious decision to . . . make the show something people care about," and the result was *The Daily Show with Jon Stewart,* a bitingly funny **satire** on the state of politics and the media. Stewart's *The Daily Show* has picked up one Emmy Award after another and has been showered with honors by everyone from the Directors Guild of America to the Television Critics Association to the Teen Choice Awards.

3   Anyone who has ever watched the show knows that Stewart doesn't take himself too seriously, and this is definitely part of his appeal. He bills himself as "the most trusted name in fake news" and promises to deliver "all the news our sponsors approve of." Sitting behind his desk offering witty comments about the day's events, he exposes the more ridiculous aspects of modern news programs in a way that makes everyone laugh. As one tagline from his show declares, "When news breaks we fix it!" During the 2004 U.S. presidential race, when mainstream news sources were soberly discussing "Decision 2004," he presented what he called "Indecision 2004."

4   Stewart's **wry** comments, fluid facial expressions, and quick wit have helped propel him to the status of cult hero among viewers aged 18–34. In fact, one poll has found that more young adults now watch the 11:00 P.M. broadcast of *The Daily Show* than watch the competing news shows on Fox, CNN, or MSNBC.

5 Stewart has not always been this successful, although many of his friends say he has always been funny. He grew up in Lawrenceville, New Jersey, where he was the only Jewish kid in town. That, coupled with his short stature (even today he stands just 5 feet 7 inches tall), made him the target of much taunting and bullying. He went to the College of William and Mary and graduated with a degree in psychology, but struggled when it came to holding down a job. He worked as a bartender, a stock boy, a pet store clerk—for a while he even did a puppet show. "I was a little lost from the age of 18 to 24," he admits, adding, "I had my midlife crisis early."

6 At last, Stewart gathered his courage and set out for New York City in hopes of becoming a stand-up comic, a bold move that to this day he cites as his proudest moment. "I might have become a bitter guy . . . complaining about how I could've been somebody. But I sold my car and moved up to New York with no job because I wanted something different. I yearned, and I went for it."

7 His first stand-up appearance was a disaster, with a rowdy crowd heckling him off the stage before he could finish his act. Still, he stuck with it, polishing his material by working the 1:45 A.M. slot—the last act of the night—at the Comedy Cellar from Sundays through Thursdays.

Skill Break
Make Inferences

Look at paragraph 6 on this page. From reading this paragraph, you can infer that *when people are unhappy with their lives, sometimes it's because they don't try for what they really want.*

What **clue** from the text supports this inference?

How does **what you already know** support this inference?

8   By the time Stewart took the Comedy Cellar stage each night, there was often no one left in the club except the staff. This meant he was free to experiment, but it also meant he didn't get paid much. "It was a lot like being in college, except with less money," he says. "It was a lot of Ramen noodles, bologna sandwiches, and staying up to 4:00 in the morning."

9   In time, Stewart's prospects—and his act—improved, he became well-known on the comedy circuit, and in 1993 he was given a chance to star in his own show on MTV. The show lasted just a few months, but it opened the door for other television opportunities and led to a six-movie deal with Miramax. Some of these movies were never completed, and those that were—*Mixed Nuts* (1994) and *Wishful Thinking* (1997)—didn't do very well. Even so, Stewart's career was on the rise, and ultimately he was offered the chance to host *The Daily Show*.

10   Although Stewart's performance on this show appears casual and lighthearted, it takes lots of preparation to pull it off, and he and his colleagues take this work seriously. "We wake up watching news, we go to bed watching news, we watch news all day long," he says. Only by staying fully informed about world events and closely examining the news coverage offered by regular news agencies is he able to turn the day's happenings into humor.

11   Even though Stewart plays his role for laughs, he does care very much about politics and presenting important issues to viewers. "We set out to **deconstruct** the process," he says, "and give people a glimpse at what we think the reality is—and while we're doing

Fun Facts

- Stewart played soccer in high school and college.
- After he got married, he and his wife legally changed both their last names to Stewart.
- His favorite baseball team is the New York Mets.
- In 2005 Stewart was named one of the 100 most influential, or powerful, people by *Time Magazine*.

Jon Stewart gestures as he makes his point on *The Daily Show.*

that, we tell jokes." The show takes timely news stories and adds moral lessons, rude humor, and silliness. He says, "We try to mix it in just the right measure so that it tastes delicious but still has enough nutrients."

12   Creating a good show is quite a difficult job, and even though Stewart finds that *The Daily Show* often falls short of his expectations, he still loves the challenge. "I am in a very fortunate position," he maintains. "There is history being made out in the world and I have the opportunity to comment on it every day."

13   Of course, it's hard to get Jon Stewart to remain serious for long, and, as many interviewers have discovered, he loves to joke not only about the show but also about himself. When asked by one reporter how he would describe himself, Stewart says, "I am a man inside a woman inside a man inside a midget." When pressed by another to describe his plans for the future, Stewart quips, "I want to breed a race of ninjas." Then when asked "when did you know you had the gift of comedy?" he responds, "When I got fired from everything else."

14   Although Stewart may avoid discussing his success, the truth is that he is one of the most talented entertainers on television. His future creations—with or without ninjas—are sure to entertain and challenge many eager fans.

A Understanding What You Read

◆ Fill in the circle next to the correct answer or write the answer.

1. *The Daily Show with Jon Stewart* is a show that presents
   - ○ A. jokes about people's weird hobbies.
   - ○ B. a humorous look at timely news stories.
   - ○ C. interviews with well-known reporters.

2. Choose from the letters below to correctly complete the following statement. Write the letters on the lines.

   On the negative side, _____, but on the positive side, _____.

   A. Stewart could experiment with his act at the Comedy Cellar.

   B. Stewart didn't make much money at the Comedy Cellar.

   C. Stewart performed to a large crowd at the Comedy Cellar.

3. Stewart prepares to do *The Daily Show* by
   - ○ A. staying up until 4:00 in the morning.
   - ○ B. talking to celebrities and politicians.
   - ○ C. watching all the latest news coverage.

4. In which paragraph did you find the information to answer question 3?

   _____

5. Which sentence **best** states the main idea of the article?
   - ○ A. Stewart moved to New York to work as a comedian.
   - ○ B. Stewart has won television awards for *The Daily Show*.
   - ○ C. Stewart is a comedian who hosts a humorous news show.

_____ Number of Correct Answers: Part A

B Making Inferences

◆ Read the paragraph below. An inference that can be made from this paragraph is that *Stewart knows just as much about what's happening in the world as serious reporters do.* Fill in the circle next to the statement that **best** supports this inference.

1.

Although Stewart's performance on this show appears casual and lighthearted, it takes lots of preparation to pull it off, and he and his colleagues take this work seriously. "We wake up watching news, we go to bed watching news, we watch news all day long," he says. Only by staying fully informed about world events and closely examining the news coverage offered by regular news agencies is he able to turn the day's happenings into humor.

○ A. The show appears casual, but it takes a lot of preparation.
○ B. He and his colleagues take their work seriously.
○ C. He closely examines news offered by regular news agencies.

◆ Reread paragraph 13 in the article. An inference you can make from this paragraph is that *it's difficult to find out accurate personal information about Stewart.* What clues from the paragraph support this inference? How does what you already know support this inference? Write the clues and what you know on the lines.

2. Clues: _____

_____

What I Know: _____

_____

_____ Number of Correct Answers: Part B

C Using Words

◆ Cross out one of the four words in each row that does **not** relate to the word in dark type.

1. parodies

amusing   copy   hide   example

2. relevant

connected   important   meaningful   secret

3. satire

exposed   required   funny   revealed

4. wry

round   witty   clever   sarcastic

5. deconstruct

study   admire   observe   examine

◆ Choose one of the words shown in dark type above. Write a sentence using the word.

6. word: _____

_____

_____

_____ Number of Correct Answers: Part C

D Writing About It

Write Interview Questions

◆ Suppose you have a chance to interview Jon Stewart. Think of **four** questions you would like to ask. Write your questions on the lines. Use the checklist on page 103 to check your work.

1. _____

_____

2. _____

_____

3. _____

_____

4. _____

_____

Lesson 5 Add your correct answers from parts A, B, and C to get your total score. Then find the percentage for your total score on the chart below. Record your percentage on the graph on page 105.

_____ Total Score for Parts A, B, and C

_____ Percentage

Total Score	1	2	3	4	5	6	7	8	9	10	11	12	13
Percentage	8	15	23	31	38	46	54	62	69	77	85	92	100

Chris Klug

A Fortunate and Grateful Athlete

Birth Name Christopher Klug

Birth Date and Place November 18, 1972; Vail, Colorado

Home Aspen, Colorado

Think About What You Know

Have you ever had to receive special help to recover from an illness? Read the article to find out how Chris Klug survived a rare disease and became an Olympic athlete.

Word Power

What do the words below tell you about the article?

degenerative something that gets worse over time and can't be stopped

transplant when an organ from one person's body is removed and put into another person's body

optimistic believing that good things will happen

drastically extremely

recipient someone who receives something

Reading Skill

Summarizing A **summary** is a shortened version of a paragraph or article written in your own words. A summary includes only the most important ideas from the text. When you read, look for key words that give information about *who, what, where, when, how,* or *why*. This information explains the important ideas. The summary of a paragraph should be logical and no more than three sentences long.

Example

   Two styles of snowboarding are freestyle and freecarve. Freestyle, with its many jumps and tricks, is especially fun to watch. Freecarve, modeled after traditional ski racing, focuses on speed. Freecarve races take place on routes with hard-packed snow. Freestyle snowboards are shorter, while freecarve boards are built longer for speed.

Two important ideas in this paragraph are *there are two styles of snowboarding* and *freestyle includes jumps and tricks*. These ideas should be included in a summary of this paragraph. What is the third important idea that should be included? Why is it important?

Chris Klug

A Fortunate and Grateful Athlete

Chris Klug didn't feel sick. In fact, the 20-year-old world-class snowboarder appeared to be the picture of health. At 6 feet 3 inches and 215 pounds, Klug loved to fly down steep slopes at breakneck speed, carving tight lines around slalom gates and claiming one victory after another in snowboarding competitions all across the country. Although he looked and felt great, a routine medical exam revealed something wrong with Klug's liver.

2   At first doctors wondered if he was hiding a drinking problem, since alcohol abuse destroys the liver. It took a year and a half for specialists to uncover what was really going on and when they did, it wasn't good news. Klug had a rare **degenerative** liver disease called primary sclerosing cholangitis, or PSC. There was no way to reverse it, no way to stop it, and in time, doctors said, Klug would require a liver **transplant** to stay alive.

3   Despite this grim diagnosis, Klug remained **optimistic,** since the doctors also told him, "You're perfectly healthy now . . . and it could go on like that for a year—it could go on like that for 20 to 30 years . . . we don't know, this disease has a mind of its own." Klug told himself that he would be one of the lucky ones and that he wouldn't need to worry about the problem until he got much older. Doctors added Klug's name to the bottom of the waiting list for a liver transplant, and Klug continued with his plans to establish himself as a top-ranked snowboarder by competing on the World Cup circuit.

4   By 1997, when Klug was 26, doctors began to see worrisome developments in Klug's bile ducts, the small tubes that carry acid from the liver to the intestines to aid digestion. These ducts were narrowing, and, although doctors were able to flush them open again, they told Klug the procedure would have to be repeated every six

months. Klug took this new development in stride, focusing on the fact that he felt great and that his snowboarding skills were getting better every day.

5   Klug was particularly excited about being chosen for the U.S. Olympic Team for 1998, the first year snowboarding was an Olympic event. Klug finished sixth in the giant slalom in these Olympics, the highest rank of any American. This was a tremendous achievement, but he still longed for a medal. He decided to set his sights on the 2002 Olympics, determined to be even stronger and more skilled after four more years of training. Long before the 2002 Olympics, however, Klug's world changed **drastically.**

6   Klug felt the first stab of fear about his condition in November 1999, as he was driving to a training camp in Salt Lake City, Utah. He heard a radio announcer report that legendary football player Walter Payton had died from complications of the same disease that Klug had. "I almost drove off the road," Klug recalls. "I pretty much broke down crying. It was really the first time I came to the realization that I could die from this."

7   Klug eventually calmed down, but he could no longer act so casually about his condition. He became increasingly concerned as he noticed new problems, such as difficulty eating and digesting food.

Skill Break

Summarizing

Look at paragraph 6 on this page. This paragraph describes Klug's feelings about his disease.

What **key words** help you find the **most important ideas** in the paragraph?

What are the **three most important ideas** in the paragraph?

8   Six months after Walter Payton's death, Klug was on a surfing trip in California when he was awakened by a pain so sharp that it felt "like a dagger or knife was stuck in my side." Klug immediately feared his liver was shutting down permanently, and when doctors examined him they confirmed this fear. Klug's name was transferred from low priority to highest priority on the transplant list, but a transplant could only occur if a healthy liver became available—and there was no way of knowing if or when that would happen. Klug could survive for a few weeks, doctors informed him, but they also said that 10 percent of the people waiting for a new liver die before a match is found.

9   As the days and weeks passed, Klug's condition worsened. He tried to work out, but at each weight-lifting session he had less strength and less stamina. He began carrying a cell phone and a beeper with him everywhere he went so doctors could notify him if a liver became available, but as he says, "More than 80,000 people are on organ donation lists. Sixteen die each day. I thought I was going to be one of them."

10   At last, on July 28, 2000, after three months at the top of the transplant list, Klug's cell phone rang. A 13-year-old boy had died in a tragic shooting accident, and the boy's mother had agreed to donate his liver, which turned out to be a match with Klug. Doctors told Klug he had six hours to get to the University of Colorado Hospital in Denver and prepare for the operation.

11   Early the next day, Klug went through the transplant operation and received his new liver. "The moment I woke up, I knew I was better," he recalls, adding, "I could just feel it." Four days after the transplant,

Fun Facts

- Klug was an All-State quarterback on his high-school football team.
- Snowboarding was a relatively new sport when 10-year-old Klug first tried it.
- His first snowboard was a plain wooden board that he strapped to his boots with duct tape.

Chris Klug skillfully weaves his snowboard around a flag during the Men's Parallel Giant Slalom event at the 2002 Winter Olympics.

Klug was released from the hospital and a couple of days after that he was out walking around, going on a trip to the zoo and to a baseball game. His spectacular comeback was completed six months later when he returned to competitive snowboarding and resumed his plans to make the 2002 Olympic team.

12   As thrilled as he was to be healthy again, Klug's happiness was subdued by his awareness that a young boy had died in order for him to live. Klug did indeed make it to the 2002 Olympics, and he did realize his dream of earning a medal by bringing home a bronze in the parallel giant slalom. That made him the first organ transplant **recipient** ever to win an Olympic medal.

13   Even in the midst of his Olympic joy, Klug was mindful of the fact that "I wouldn't be here if not for the donor family," and in some ways the most important moment for him came shortly after his Olympic victory, when he was introduced to his donor family for the first time.

14   Klug's liver had come from a boy named Billy Flood who, ironically, had always wanted to snowboard but had never had the money to do so. Klug showed Flood's family his Olympic medal and told them, "I'm wearing this around my neck . . . because of them and their decision. I told them they were my heroes."

A Understanding What You Read

◆ Fill in the circle next to the correct answer.

1. From what the article told you about primary sclerosing cholangitis, you can conclude that it is
   ○ A. very familiar to most doctors.
   ○ B. not caused by alcohol abuse.
   ○ C. common among male athletes.

2. When Klug found out he had PSC he
   ○ A. didn't think he would get sick until he was much older.
   ○ B. still hadn't become a world-class snowboarder.
   ○ C. began crying and almost drove his car off the road.

3. Which of the following statements is an opinion rather than a fact?
   ○ A. It took a year and a half to uncover what was wrong.
   ○ B. He was chosen for the U.S. Olympic Team.
   ○ C. This was a tremendous achievement.

4. Klug met his donor family for the first time
   ○ A. a few weeks after his transplant operation.
   ○ B. shortly after he won the Olympic bronze medal.
   ○ C. six months after the news of Walter Payton's death.

5. From the information in the article you can predict that
   ○ A. Klug will keep in touch with the Flood family.
   ○ B. Klug will get a special award for his courage.
   ○ C. Klug will not have any more health concerns.

_____ Number of Correct Answers: Part A

B Summarizing

◆ Read the paragraph below. Underline the key words and phrases that explain the most important ideas. Then fill in the circle next to the statement that **best** summarizes the paragraph.

1.

Despite this grim diagnosis, Klug remained optimistic, since the doctors also told him, "You're perfectly healthy now . . . and it could go on like that for a year—it could go on like that for 20 to 30 years . . . we don't know, this disease has a mind of its own." Klug told himself that he would be one of the lucky ones and that he wouldn't need to worry about the problem until he got much older. Doctors added Klug's name to the bottom of the waiting list for a liver transplant, and Klug continued with his plans to establish himself as a top-ranked snowboarder by competing on the World Cup circuit.

○ A. Klug was optimistic and told himself that he would be one of the lucky ones. He kept his plans to train to become a top-ranked snowboarder on the World Cup circuit.

○ B. Doctors gave Klug a grim diagnosis and said they didn't know what would happen with his disease. They said that Klug was healthy and could stay that way for 20 to 30 years.

○ C. Klug kept a positive outlook because doctors told him he could stay healthy for a long time. He got his name on the list for a liver transplant and continued competing as a snowboarder.

◆ Reread paragraph 9 in the article. Write the **three most important ideas** in the paragraph on the lines. Then write a summary of the paragraph in two or three sentences.

2. Most Important Ideas: _____

Summary:_____

_____ Number of Correct Answers: Part B

C Using Words

◆ Complete each sentence with a word from the box. Write the missing word on the line.

degenerative	optimistic	recipient
transplant	drastically	

1. Last year she was the _____ of the Spanish Club award.

2. Transferring to a new school _____ changed my social life.

3. The first successful heart _____ surgery made medical history.

4. The increasing weakness in his legs was the result of a

_____ disease.

5. The sunny weather made me _____ about the day ahead.

◆ Choose one of the words from the box. Write a new sentence using the word.

6. word: _____

_____

_____ Number of Correct Answers: Part C

D Writing About It

Write an Advertisement

◆ Suppose Chris Klug is coming to your school to give a talk. Write an advertisement for this event that describes Chris Klug and his career. Write **at least four** sentences. Use the checklist on page 103 to check your work.

Coming to Our School: Snowboarder Chris Klug

_____

_____

_____

_____

_____

_____

Lesson 6 Add your correct answers from parts A, B, and C to get your total score. Then find the percentage for your total score on the chart below. Record your percentage on the graph on page 105.

_____ Total Score for Parts A, B, and C

_____ Percentage

Total Score	1	2	3	4	5	6	7	8	9	10	11	12	13
Percentage	8	15	23	31	38	46	54	62	69	77	85	92	100

Compare and Contrast

◆ Think about the celebrities in Unit Two. Pick two articles that tell about celebrities who were positive about their future. Use information from the articles to fill in this chart.

Celebrity's Name		
What did the celebrity feel positive about?		
What did the celebrity do because of these positive feelings?		
Did things turn out as well as the celebrity expected? Explain.		

Antonio Banderas

Terrence Howard

Lynne Cox

Antonio Banderas

Making It Big in Hollywood

Birth Name José Antonio Domínguez Bandera

Birth Date and Place August 10, 1960; Málaga, Spain

Home Los Angeles, California

Think About What You Know

What commitments have you made in your life? How do you keep these commitments? Read the article to find out about Antonio Banderas and his strong commitment to his acting career.

Word Power

What do the words below tell you about the article?

dissuade to persuade someone not to do something

dubbed to change the original language of a film into another language

phonetically by focusing on the specific sounds in words or speech

intensive involving a great deal of concentration and effort over a short time

overshadow to make something seem less important than something else

Reading Skill

Problem and Solution Authors often describe **problems** and **solutions** in their writing. A problem is a situation that causes difficulties. A solution is a way to solve the problem. Taking note of the problems and solutions as you read can help improve your overall understanding of the text.

Example

> My sister always wanted to be an artist. When she was younger, she spent all of her time drawing and often neglected her schoolwork. When she realized that her grades might not be good enough to get into a college art program, she started putting more time and effort into her regular studies. It must have worked, because last year she was accepted into a great college art program.

The paragraph shows a problem and a solution. The problem is that *the sister's grades might not be good enough to get into a college art program.* What was the solution? How did this solve the problem?

Antonio Banderas

Making It Big in Hollywood

When Antonio Banderas was growing up in Málaga, Spain, he dreamed of becoming a professional soccer player. But a broken foot at age 14 effectively ended that fantasy and forced Banderas to search for a new passion. He found it when his parents, who usually exposed him only to classical theater, took him to see a local production of the American musical *Hair* (1974). By intermission, Banderas had concluded that his destiny lay in acting and nothing, not even the strong disapproval of his conservative parents, could **dissuade** him.

2 Banderas began spending hours in front of his family's little black-and-white television set watching old Hollywood movies that were **dubbed** in Spanish and soon signed on with a local theater where he performed in street shows. "While other kids were into rock and roll . . . I was all theater, theater, theater," he recalls. He also enrolled in Málaga's School of Dramatic Art where, he says, "we were always in the truck, traveling from little village to little village, performing. You learned to do everything—scenery, costumes, makeup, and lights. It was wonderful."

3 Banderas's parents hoped that their son would soon tire of the grim realities of small-time acting, but the experience merely increased his enthusiasm and commitment to his craft. In 1980 at the age of 19, Banderas moved to Madrid hoping to make a name for himself as an actor, but with no money in the bank he had to take whatever employment he could find, from waiter in a pub to salesclerk in a department store. "The money I earned went to buy decent clothes for auditions and to pay for acting lessons," he says. "I remember when I couldn't even afford to take the bus, so I had to walk six miles to get to an audition. As I walked, I'd look between the parked cars, hoping to find some change that someone might have dropped."

4   Banderas's fortune improved when he auditioned for—and was awarded—a spot in Spain's prestigious National Theater, and he got another big break in 1982 when an ambitious young director named Pedro Almodovar cast him in the film *Labyrinth of Passion.* From there, Banderas went on to build a solid reputation as one of Spain's finest actors, one who was unafraid to stretch his skills by taking even the most outrageous roles. Still, he says, "whether they admit it or not, every European actor wants to be in the American movies," and he was no exception.

5   So when Banderas got a call to audition for the part of a Cuban immigrant in the Hollywood movie *The Mambo Kings* (1992), he was thrilled. There was, however, one problem: Banderas didn't speak a word of English. Desperate not to let this opportunity pass him by, he flew to Hollywood for a screen test and studied his lines **phonetically,** syllable by syllable, until he could pronounce them correctly. His strategy worked—he got the role—and although the movie was only a moderate success, it brought Banderas into the consciousness of U.S. moviegoers and launched his Hollywood movie career.

6   Banderas knew his future in Hollywood would be severely limited if he didn't learn English, so he began an **intensive** language program that had him studying eight hours a day. He soon learned to speak English fluently, although he still spoke with a heavy Spanish accent.

Skill Break

Problem and Solution

Look at paragraph 5 on this page. This paragraph describes a problem and a solution. The problem was that Banderas wanted to audition for a Hollywood movie but he didn't speak any English. What was the **solution?**

How did this **solve the problem?**

7   In 1993 he appeared with Tom Hanks in the Academy-Award winning movie *Philadelphia,* a movie that pushed Banderas into the Hollywood spotlight and brought him a flood of new film offers. Thrilled with his rising movie career, he jumped into one production after another with promises of more to come.

8   Although his career was flourishing, Banderas paid a high personal price for this success. For eight years he had been married to Spanish actress Ana Leza, a woman who had so captured his heart when they first met that he had written her love poems and composed songs for her. Banderas had always been devoted to his wife, but she didn't share his love for America. She had initially accompanied him to most of his movie sets in the United States, but in time she began to stay in Spain to pursue her own interests when her husband went to work in Hollywood. As a result, Banderas and his wife started to drift apart.

9   In 1995 Banderas started filming *Two Much* opposite Melanie Griffith, and their relationship was soon a popular topic of discussion in the gossip columns. What followed was a very messy, very public breakup for Griffith and actor Don Johnson, her husband at the time, and a similarly ugly end to Banderas's marriage with Ana Leza.

10   For a time it appeared that the negative publicity about what Banderas was doing in his personal life might **overshadow** his career, turn the public against him, and make directors reluctant to work with him—but that didn't happen. Instead Banderas and Griffith cemented their commitment to each other in 1996 by getting married and having a daughter, whom they named Stella. Banderas settled down with his new family (which included Griffith's two children from previous marriages) and refocused on his acting career, starring in numerous hits such as *Evita* (1996) and *The Mask of Zorro* (1998).

Fun Facts

▶ Banderas enjoys playing practical jokes on people.

▶ His friends in Spain nicknamed him Lucky.

▶ He has a cat named Oliver.

▶ He is a big fan of the movie *Shrek* and has seen it at least six times.

In 2005 Antonio Banderas starred in a second Zorro film, *The Legend of Zorro*.

11   By 2003 Banderas had made dozens of films and was ready to revisit his roots by returning to live theater. For years he had avoided Broadway because, as he says, "I was afraid of doing theater in English," but he finally decided the time was right and agreed to star in the Broadway show *Nine*.

12   As Banderas was about to make his Broadway debut, he was a nervous wreck, later commenting, "When I first came to New York . . . I remember not being able to call room service because I was afraid of speaking English. So imagine what I felt the night we opened this show when I was in the wings thinking, 'I have to speak for two and a half hours in English and sing 12 songs.'" He was, he says, "sweating like an idiot." Everything went smoothly, however, and Banderas earned excellent reviews for his performance.

13   The following year, Banderas took on yet another challenge when he provided the voice for Puss in Boots in the animated smash hit *Shrek 2*. However, the real highlight of his career might have been in 2005, when Antonio Banderas was given the ultimate symbol of recognition for an actor—his own star on Hollywood's renowned Walk of Fame. The young actor, who had set out with nothing but talent, enthusiasm, and drive, had become a celebrated and honored Hollywood star.

A Understanding What You Read

◆ Fill in the circle next to the correct answer.

1. What caused Banderas to start watching his family's little black-and-white television set all the time?

- ○ A. He wanted to learn about acting and making movies.
- ○ B. His parents did not want to buy a color television.
- ○ C. He needed to pass the time while his foot was healing.

2. When Banderas first moved to Madrid, he was so poor that he

- ○ A. took the bus everywhere he went.
- ○ B. looked for spare change in the streets.
- ○ C. couldn't afford to go to auditions.

3. The movie that first brought Banderas many new movie offers was

- ○ A. *The Mask of Zorro.*
- ○ B. *Philadelphia.*
- ○ C. *Two Much.*

4. How is Banderas an example of someone with commitment and dedication?

- ○ A. He is from Spain, but he played a Cuban immigrant.
- ○ B. He fell in love with his costar, Melanie Griffith.
- ○ C. He stayed with acting even though he had to struggle.

5. The author probably wrote this article in order to

- ○ A. inform the reader about one actor's inspiring career.
- ○ B. explain to the reader how actors get their roles.
- ○ C. convince the reader to see more Hollywood movies.

_____ Number of Correct Answers: Part A

B Understanding Problem and Solution

◆ Read the paragraph below. The paragraph describes a problem and a solution. Fill in the circle next to the sentence that **best** describes the **problem**.

1.

When Antonio Banderas was growing up in Málaga, Spain, he dreamed of becoming a professional soccer player. But a broken foot at age 14 effectively ended that fantasy and forced Banderas to search for a new passion. He found it when his parents, who usually exposed him only to classical theater, took him to see a local production of the American musical *Hair* (1974). By intermission, Banderas had concluded that his destiny lay in acting and nothing, not even the strong disapproval of his conservative parents, could dissuade him.

○ A. Banderas could no longer play soccer.
○ B. Banderas saw only classical theater.
○ C. Banderas had conservative parents.

◆ Reread the paragraph above. What was the **solution** to the problem? How did this solve the problem? Write the solution and how it solved the problem on the lines.

2. Solution: _____

_____

How It Solved the Problem: _____

_____

_____ Number of Correct Answers: Part B

C   Using Words

◆ The words and phrases in the list below relate to the words in the box. Some words or phrases in the list have a meaning that is the same or similar to a word in the box. Some have the opposite meaning. Write the related word from the box on each line. Use each word from the box twice.

dissuade	phonetically	overshadow
dubbed	intensive	

Same or similar meaning

1. rerecorded _____

2. dominate _____

3. by sound _____

4. advise against _____

5. condensed _____

6. by spoken word _____

7. voiced over _____

Opposite meaning

8. casual _____

9. highlight _____

10. encourage _____

_____ Number of Correct Answers: Part C

D Writing About It

Write a Story

◆ Write a story about Banderas. Tell about about the beginning of his acting career. Explain how he decided to become an actor and how he became well known in Spain. Write **at least four** sentences. Use the checklist on page 103 to check your work.

_____

_____

_____

_____

_____

_____

_____

_____

Lesson 7 Add your correct answers from parts A, B, and C to get your total score. Then find the percentage for your total score on the chart below. Record your percentage on the graph on page 105.

_____ Total Score for Parts A, B, and C

_____ Percentage

Total Score	1	2	3	4	5	6	7	8	9	10	11	12	13	14	15	16	17
Percentage	6	12	18	24	29	35	41	47	53	59	65	70	76	82	88	94	100

Terrence Howard

The Long Road to Fame

Birth Name Terrence Dashon Howard

Birth Date and Place March 11, 1969; Chicago, Illinois

Home Philadelphia, Pennsylvania

Think About What You Know

Do you know what it's like to work hard and do well but then not be appreciated for your efforts? Read the article to find out how Terrence Howard finally gained popular recognition for his acting talent.

Word Power

What do the words below tell you about the article?

consistently showing the same behavior or abilities time after time

infuse to fill something with a certain feeling or quality

subtleties qualities that are important but not easy to see or understand

eschews intentionally avoids something

vulnerability a state of being undefended and easily harmed

Reading Skill

Make Inferences Authors don't always say everything they want the reader to understand. Sometimes authors hint at what they mean by providing clues. Good readers **make inferences.** To make an inference, use the author's clues and your own knowledge or experiences to fill in information about the people, places, and events described in the text.

Example

My cousin is studying drama. She is very serious about becoming an actor. She knows that most working actors aren't famous, and many actors never become rich, but she is still excited about pursuing a career in acting.

One thing that the reader can infer from this paragraph is that *the cousin's desire to be an actor is greater than her desire for money.* A clue that supports this inference is "she knows that . . . many actors never become rich." How does what you already know support this inference?

Terrence Howard

The Long Road to Fame

For years Terrence Howard had been one of the most underappreciated actors in Hollywood. Although he had appeared in many Hollywood movies, the average moviegoer had never even heard of him. Despite this lack of public recognition, the directors, critics, and movie-industry experts knew him well. They **consistently** praised him for the intensity and passion he brought to his work, using words such as "brilliant," "fantastic," and "gifted." One critic called him "an actor you absolutely cannot take your eyes off." Another described him as "a fearless performer, taking on roles and enthusiastically tackling characters a meeker man would avoid." Howard was "the sleeping giant of supporting players" or, as one entertainment writer put it, "the best actor you've never heard of."

2   All of that changed in 2005, however, when two of his movies—*Crash* and *Hustle & Flow*—finally propelled him to the forefront of public awareness. In *Crash* he portrays a successful Hollywood director humiliated by a racist police officer. In *Hustle & Flow* he plays a street hustler who suffers a personal crisis and decides to pursue a career as a rapper. Both films won praise from the critics. Howard's performances in these films were so masterful that many people began comparing him to legendary film greats such as Marlon Brando and Denzel Washington.

3   Although Howard was grateful for the recognition of his acting talent, he was determined not to be overcome by all the hype. As he modestly pointed out, "I've been at it 18 years. It's about time my investment started to show interest."

4   Howard's slow climb toward stardom began back in the late 1980s, but by that time he had already survived a difficult childhood. Howard's earliest years were spent in the suburbs of Cleveland, where his father was an insurance agent, but when Howard was three, a life-altering event occurred.

5   One afternoon at a department store, Howard's father found himself caught in a racially charged encounter that left a man dead. As a result, Howard's father was sent to prison. The family, unable to afford their suburban home any longer, had to move into a less expensive—and more dangerous—section of Cleveland. Although Howard's father was eventually released from prison, the family broke up, and both of Howard's parents went on to start new families, with Howard splitting his time between them.

6   When his mother moved to California, he and his brothers stayed in Cleveland with their father, even though that meant dealing with their very hostile stepmother. As Howard recalls, "My dad moved us into a house when I was 16 years old to live and support ourselves because my stepmom wanted to shoot us." He adds that "in the wintertime we didn't have any electricity because we couldn't pay for it." Howard remembers using a kerosene heater to keep from freezing and "trying to be warm and trying to wash up because all the pipes are frozen in the house . . . you put a pot on top of the kerosene container so you would have hot water to wash up . . . that was my life from 16 to 18 years old in Cleveland."

7   When Howard finished high school, he decided to move to New York City, where he had spent some summers as a child. Although he had never pursued theater or drama before, he started dreaming of an acting career and began pressing casting directors for auditions. After many long, hard months, he began to get small roles in various television shows and movies.

Skill Break
Make Inferences

Look at paragraph 7 on this page. The paragraph describes how Howard got started in acting. From reading this paragraph you can infer that *Howard has natural acting talent.*

What **clues** from the text supports this inference?

How does **what you already know** support this inference?

8   Throughout the 1990s and early 2000s, he had steady work as an actor, being cast in many supporting roles, but was never offered a starring part. While he never played a lead, he managed to **infuse** his secondary characters with depth and humanity. He exploited their ability to help shape and define the lead characters. Although various directors and producers assured him that he was destined for stardom, he learned not to take these assurances too seriously, saying, "I've been the next big thing in this business for a few years."

9   One obstacle that kept Howard from receiving bigger roles was his reputation for being difficult. He admits that whenever he felt he was being treated with disrespect, "the claws would come out," and he would verbally lash out. He points out that it's not uncommon for actors with high standards to be labeled "difficult" and says, "Al Pacino, Marlon Brando, Glenn Close, Angela Bassett . . . everybody I respected was labeled difficult. I'm not that way because I want only green and red M&M's. I'm difficult because I want to act the truth."

10   When Howard was finally offered a starring role—that of DJay in *Hustle & Flow*—he was reluctant to accept it because it meant playing a drug-dealing street hustler. He didn't want to reinforce the image of African Americans as criminals and drug lords. "I fought against this role for a long time because I am a father of three and don't want this to be my legacy," he explains. When he read the script, however, he was impressed by the emotional honesty of the lead character. He realized that, like all the other characters he had brought to life over the years, this character had **subtleties** to be revealed and a story worth telling.

Fun Facts

- Howard taught himself to play both piano and guitar.
- He prefers country music over rap music.
- His great-grandmother, Minnie Gentry, was a stage actor.
- He enjoys restoring old houses.

Terrence Howard is all smiles at the screening of *Hustle & Flow* at the Sundance Film Festival.

11   Today, although Howard has broken into the upper levels of stardom, he continues to stand slightly apart from the typical celebrity crowd. He **eschews** the Hollywood lifestyle, preferring a quiet existence in Philadelphia to life in the fast lane of Los Angeles. "I tried to live in Los Angeles," he says, "but I just existed there." He chose Philadelphia, he says, because it's his wife's home town and "I wanted to get back to where people were real, where a smile is a smile, not a trick pulled out of a sleeve."

12   Howard showed his independent streak again when he refused to pose for the cover of *Jet* magazine to promote the movie *Hustle & Flow*. The magazine's policy against featuring white people on the cover meant that his white costar, Taryn Manning, would be excluded. He knew his decision would anger some people, but he didn't care. "Anything where the whole cast is not included, I'm not participating in it," he says.

13   Howard's outsider attitude may alienate a few individuals, but chances are that most people will admire him for his honesty and integrity. However, even if they don't, they have to admire the depth, **vulnerability,** and power that he brings to his work on screen.

◆ Fill in the circle next to the correct answer.

1. During the first 18 years of his acting career, Howard
   ○ A. moved to Hollywood and appeared in *Jet* magazine.
   ○ B. lived with his brother and could not pay for heat.
   ○ C. played supporting roles and received great reviews.

2. Which of the following statements is an opinion rather than a fact?
   ○ A. Howard is often a difficult actor to work with.
   ○ B. Howard moved to New York after high school.
   ○ C. Howard has been compared to Marlon Brando.

3. Howard chooses to live in Philadelphia instead of Hollywood because
   ○ A. he prefers a quiet life where people are real.
   ○ B. people in Hollywood don't understand him.
   ○ C. he wants his family to be safe from crime.

4. From the information in the article, you can predict that
   ○ A. Howard will move back to Los Angeles.
   ○ B. Howard will be offered more lead roles.
   ○ C. Howard will play a criminal in another movie.

5. Which sentence **best** describes the lesson about life that this article teaches?
   ○ A. Wealth comes from working hard and spending wisely.
   ○ B. Truth and integrity are more valuable than fame.
   ○ C. If you don't do well at one thing, try something new.

_____ Number of Correct Answers: Part A

B Making Inferences

◆ Read the paragraph below. An inference that can be made from this paragraph is that *Howard's father may have been wrongly accused and imprisoned.* Fill in the circle next to the statement that **best** supports this inference.

1.

One afternoon at a department store, Howard's father found himself caught in a racially charged encounter that left a man dead. As a result, Howard's father was sent to prison. The family, unable to afford their suburban home any longer, had to move into a less expensive—and more dangerous—section of Cleveland. Although Howard's father was eventually released from prison, the family broke up, and both of Howard's parents went on to start new families, with Howard splitting his time between them.

○ A. Howard's father found himself caught in a racially charged encounter.
○ B. Howard's father was sent to prison.
○ C. Howard's family broke up, and his father started a new family.

◆ Reread paragraph 6 in the article. An inference you can make from this paragraph is that *at least one of Howard's brothers must have been old enough to be responsible for Howard.* What clues support this inference? How does what you already know support this inference? Write the clues and what you know on the lines.

2. Clues: _____

What I Know: _____

_____

_____ Number of Correct Answers: Part B

C Using Words

◆ Complete the analogies below by writing a word from the box on each line. Remember that in an analogy, the last two words or phrases must be related in the same way that the first two are related.

consistently	subtleties	vulnerability
infuse	eschews	

1. regular : normal :: lack of protection : _____

2. rise : fall :: seeks : _____

3. bend : straighten :: drain : _____

4. yelling : whispering :: rarely : _____

5. strong : steel :: hidden : _____

◆ Choose one of the words from the box. Write a sentence using the word.

6. word: _____

_____

_____

_____ Number of Correct Answers: Part C

D Writing About It

Write a Magazine Article

◆ Suppose you are an arts and entertainment reporter. Write a magazine article about Terrence Howard's acting career. Write **at least four** sentences. Use the checklist on page 103 to check your work.

_____

_____

_____

_____

_____

_____

_____

_____

Lesson 8 Add your correct answers from parts A, B, and C to get your total score. Then find the percentage for your total score on the chart below. Record your percentage on the graph on page 105.

_____ Total Score for Parts A, B, and C

_____ Percentage

Total Score	1	2	3	4	5	6	7	8	9	10	11	12	13
Percentage	8	15	23	31	38	46	54	62	69	77	85	92	100

Lynne Cox

Extreme Swimmer

Birth Name Lynne Elaine Cox

Birth Date and Place January 2, 1957; Boston, Massachusetts

Home Los Alamitos, California

Think About What You Know

Have you ever gone swimming in a lake, river, or ocean that was really cold? How did it feel when you first jumped into the water? Read the article to find out about Lynne Cox and her amazing Antarctic swim.

Word Power

What do the words below tell you about the article?

culmination an event or result that happens after a long period of work

anomaly something that is very different from what is usual or normal

extremities the parts of the body that are farthest away from the torso, such as the feet and hands

inhospitable difficult to live in because of harsh weather or lack of shelter

hyperventilating breathing too quickly and too deeply, often causing dizziness

Reading Skill

Summarizing A **summary** is a shortened version of a paragraph or an article written in your own words. Good summaries include only the most important ideas from the text. The summary of a paragraph should be logical and no more than three sentences long.

Example

Antarctica is a continent that covers the globe's South Pole. Almost all the land is covered in ice. It is the coldest place on earth. In fact, the coldest temperature ever documented in Antarctica was minus 129 degrees Fahrenheit. Scientists are studying Antarctica to get more information about global climate changes. The thick Antarctic ice holds a record of these changes that goes back at least 650,000 years.

Two important ideas in this paragraph are *Antarctica is a continent located at the South Pole* and *it is the coldest place on earth.* These two ideas should be included in a summary of this paragraph. What is the third important idea that should be included in the summary?

Lynne Cox

Extreme Swimmer

No one in the history of the world had ever done what Lynne Cox was about to do—or even attempted it. Over the years, Cox had completed some amazing swims. She'd swum across the treacherous English Channel in record time, been stalked by a shark while swimming around Africa's Cape of Good Hope, and raced across the filthy brown water of the Nile River—but this was an extreme adventure even by her standards. The 45-year-old planned to swim a mile in the freezing-cold water of the Antarctic Sea, which averages about the same temperature as a bathtub full of melting ice cubes.

2   In water that cold, explains Professor William Keatinge of the University of London, "the whole beating of the heart goes completely adrift," causing cardiac arrest and death. Most people wouldn't survive five minutes in such water. Yet not only did Cox plan a 25-minute Antarctic swim, but she also planned to do it without a wetsuit to insulate her from the cold and without any sort of cage to shield her from the aggressive leopard seals and unpredictable killer whales that inhabit that region of the world.

3   Why would any rational person embark on such a journey? For Cox, it would be the **culmination** of 30 years' worth of exotic swims, swims she had undertaken for two reasons: first, to help build bridges between different groups of people, as when she swam from Egypt to Israel in support of peace in the Middle East, and second, to test the limits of human endurance, as when she became the first woman to swim the turbulent Cook Strait in New Zealand.

4   Prior to the Antarctic endeavor, Cox's most impressive feat was a two-hour swim across the Bering Strait, the waterway separating Alaska from Russia. Since the water of the Bering Strait averages a chilling 40 degrees Fahrenheit, experts had feared that she would die from cardiac arrest or hypothermia, but she completed the swim

without becoming ill. Although her core body temperature did drop significantly as she swam, it returned to normal soon after she emerged from the water.

5 Cox's ability to survive such a swim makes her a medical **anomaly,** and scientists have spent years trying to determine how she does it. They have uncovered several factors that contribute to her success. First, at 5 feet 6 inches and 180 pounds, Cox is well insulated from the harsh temperature of the water by a layer of fat evenly distributed throughout her body. Secondly, her body density is precisely that of seawater, so she neither floats nor sinks and thus can maintain her position near the surface of the water without expending energy. In addition, scientists have discovered that her body has an astounding ability to maintain its core temperature. When Cox enters cold water, her body shuts down the flow of blood to the **extremities,** where it would be cooled by the surrounding water, and redirects it to the vital organs to keep them warm and functional for astonishingly long periods of time.

6 Even for Cox, however, Antarctica would be a supreme challenge. No one knew if any human could survive a swim in such an **inhospitable** environment. Cox trained vigorously, adding 12 pounds for extra insulation and increasing her already-impressive upper body strength. She grew her hair long so it would trap body heat inside her bathing cap and had her teeth sealed to prevent them from shattering in the extreme cold. Then, in November 2002, she sailed to Admiralty Bay, Antarctica, accompanied by a host of doctors, navigators, and photographers.

Skill Break

Summarizing

Look at paragraph 5 on this page. This paragraph describes Cox's unusual physical characteristics.

What are the **four most important ideas** that you would include in a summary of this paragraph?

What information would you **leave out** of the summary?

7   Cox wanted to make a brief practice swim before her official attempt, so one calm day she donned her bathing suit, bathing cap, and goggles and immersed herself in the near-freezing water. "The water was searingly cold," Cox recalls. She also says that "the water felt different from any other water I'd swum in, as if it were more solid than fluid, as though I were swimming through a liquid [snow cone]." After a few minutes she got out, her entire body shaking uncontrollably from the cold.

8   A few days later, on December 15, 2002, Cox again entered the frigid water and commenced a longer swim, this time determined to cover a full mile. The water and air temperature were hovering at 32 degrees Fahrenheit, and the wind was gusting at about 35 miles per hour. When Cox first entered the water, it didn't feel quite as bitterly cold as she expected. "I didn't realize then that the nerves on my skin's surface had been damaged from the first swim," she says. "I didn't know that the nerves that signaled danger weren't firing."

9   Quickly, however, the cold penetrated her skin and reached her muscles with an intensity that was "as sharp as broken glass." She began **hyperventilating** and felt waves of panic threatening to engulf her. "My brain wasn't working as it normally did," she says, although she doesn't know if that was because she was overwhelmed by the sensations her body was experiencing or because her blood and oxygen were rushing to her muscles to keep them functioning. In any case, it took all her concentration to bring her breathing under control and keep her arms and legs moving.

Fun Facts

▶ Cox has worked with instructors in the U.S. Navy to teach them what she knows about cold-water survival.

▶ She has worked as a librarian, a swimming instructor, and a writer.

▶ She wrote a book called *Swimming to Antarctica.*

Lynne Cox swam in freezing-cold waters wearing only a bathing suit, cap, and goggles.

10   With grim determination and barely controlled panic, she took breath after breath and stroke after stroke until at last, after 21 minutes in the water, she approached the shore of Antarctica. Suddenly a group of penguins plunged into the water and swam over to join her. "They zoomed under me in bursts of speed," she later wrote. "One cannonballed off a ledge, another slipped on some ice and belly flopped, and three penguins swam within inches of my hands . . . I had no idea why they were swimming with me, but I knew it was a good sign; it meant there were no killer whales or leopard seals in the area." The penguins stayed with Cox during the waning minutes of what turned out to be a 1.22-mile swim.

11   Although Cox's core temperature had gone down to 95.5 degrees by the time she reached shore, it soon bounced back to normal after she left the water. Eventually the nerves in her skin healed as well. Upon hearing of her success, some people hailed her as a hero and others merely shook their heads in disbelief, but everyone had to admit that with this remarkable swim, Lynne Cox had achieved her goal. She had tested the limits of human endurance and "expanded the notion of the possible."

A Understanding What You Read

Fill in the circle next to the correct answer or write the answer.

1. An average person attempting an Antarctic swim would probably

- ○ A. suffer cardiac arrest.
- ○ B. be attacked by sharks.
- ○ C. swim only one mile.

2. Prior to her Antarctic swim, Cox gained cold-water swimming experience when she swam across the

- ○ A. English Channel.
- ○ B. Bering Strait.
- ○ C. Cook Strait.

3. Choose from the letters below to correctly complete the following statement. Write the letters on the lines.

On the positive side, _____, but on the negative side, _____.

A. Cox again entered the frigid water and started a longer swim

B. the nerves on her skin had been damaged from the first swim

C. the water didn't feel as bitterly cold as Cox had expected

4. In which paragraph did you find your information to answer question 3?

_____

5. If you were stranded on a small raft in the icy waters of Antarctica, how could you use the information in the article to help you survive?

- ○ A. I would avoid killer whales by staying close to penguins.
- ○ B. I would jump in the water and swim toward the shore.
- ○ C. I would breathe quickly and very deeply to stay warm.

_____ Number of Correct Answers: Part A

92

B Summarizing

◆ Read the paragraph below. Then read the sentences below the paragraph. Write the letter *I* on the lines next to the **three** sentences that contain the most important ideas from the paragraph.

1.

Why would any rational person embark on such a journey? For Cox, it would be the culmination of 30 years' worth of exotic swims, swims she had undertaken for two reasons: first, to help build bridges between different groups of people, as when she swam from Egypt to Israel in support of peace in the Middle East, and second, to test the limits of human endurance, as when she became the first woman to swim the turbulent Cook Strait in New Zealand.

_____ Cox had 30 years' worth of swimming experience.

_____ Cox had two reasons for undertaking her exotic swims.

_____ She wanted to help build bridges between people.

_____ She swam from Egypt to Israel in support of peace.

_____ She wanted to test the limits of human endurance.

◆ Use the **three most important** ideas that you selected above to write a summary of the paragraph in your own words. Your summary should be **no more than three** sentences long.

2. _____

_____

_____

_____ Number of Correct Answers: Part B

C Using Words

◆ Cross out one of the four words in each row that does **not** relate to the word in dark type.

1. culmination

result   unknown   important   effort

2. anomaly

odd   irregular   large   rare

3. extremities

outer   tip   ends   loose

4. inhospitable

cold   extreme   uncomfortable   imaginary

5. hyperventilating

lungs   air   shape   speed

◆ Choose one of the words shown in dark type above. Write a sentence using the word.

6. word: _____

_____

_____

_____ Number of Correct Answers: Part C

Write a Comic Strip

◆ Write a comic strip about Lynne Cox's Antarctic swim. Look at what is happening in each scene. Then write **at least two** sentences in each bubble. Use the checklist on page 103 to check your work.

Lesson 9 Add your correct answers from parts A, B, and C to get your total score. Then find the percentage for your total score on the chart below. Record your percentage on the graph on page 105.

_____ Total Score for Parts A, B, and C

_____ Percentage

Total Score	1	2	3	4	5	6	7	8	9	10	11	12	13
Percentage	8	15	23	31	38	46	54	62	69	77	85	92	100

Compare and Contrast

◆ Think about the celebrities in Unit Three. Pick two articles that tell about celebrities whose past experience led to bigger success. Use information from the articles to fill in this chart.

Celebrity's Name		
What success did the celebrity have?		
What kind of past experience did the celebrity have?		
How do you think this past experience helped prepare the celebrity for success?		

Glossary

A

adversity   a situation that brings a lot of problems or hardships   p. 39

alluded   talked about something indirectly   p. 6

anomaly   something that is very different from what is usual or normal   p. 89

aptitude   a natural skill or ability to learn   p. 14

assimilate   to take in, absorb, and use in the body   p. 26

B

backlash   a strong reaction by a number of people against an event
or a decision   p. 38

C

charisma   the ability to easily attract other people and get them to like you   p. 15

compensate   to do something that balances out the effect of a weakness
or a loss   p. 6

composure   calmness   p. 39

conformity   behavior that follows the same rules or ideas that are accepted
by most other people in society   p. 14

consistently   showing the same behavior or abilities time after time   p. 78

culmination   an event or result that happens after a long period of work   p. 88

D

deconstruct to analyze something with the belief that there is no single explanation or meaning p. 48

degenerative something that gets worse over time and can't be stopped p. 56

diagnosis the process of looking at a person closely to find out what is wrong with them p. 27

dissuade to persuade someone not to do something p. 68

drastically extremely p. 57

dubbed to change the original language of a film into another language p. 68

E

eluded escaped someone's understanding p. 24

eschews intentionally avoids something p. 81

euphoria a feeling of extreme joy and excitement p. 27

extremities the parts of the body that are farthest away from the torso, such as the feet and hands p. 89

H

hyperventilating breathing too quickly and too deeply, often causing dizziness p. 90

I

individuality the qualities that make a person different from others p. 14

infuse to fill something with a certain feeling or quality p. 80

inhospitable difficult to live in because of harsh weather or lack of shelter p. 89

intensive   involving a great deal of concentration and effort over a
short time   p. 69

N

nutritionist   someone who knows the right foods to eat for
good health   p. 25

O

optimistic   believing that good things will happen   p. 56

overshadow   to make something seem less important than something else   p. 70

P

parodies   imitations of something or someone that are done in a
humorous way   p. 46

perception   the ideas that a person has formed about something   p. 38

persevered   kept on trying to do something in a determined way despite
difficulties   p. 37

phonetically   by focusing on the specific sounds in words or speech   p. 69

R

recipient   someone who receives something   p. 59

relevant   directly relating to a current issue or topic of discussion   p. 46

ridicule   to laugh at someone or say things to make someone feel foolish   p. 4

rivalries   two or more people competing for one thing, especially when they
have been competing for a long time   p. 7

S

satire   a way of criticizing something or someone using humor, so that their faults can be seen more clearly   p. 46

subtleties   qualities that are important but not easy to see or understand   p. 80

surname   the name that a person shares with his or her family; in English it is the person's last name   p. 14

T

transplant   when an organ from one person's body is removed and put into another person's body   p. 56

U

underestimating   thinking that someone is not as good or talented as they really are   p. 7

V

vulnerability   a state of being undefended and easily harmed   p. 81

W

wry   knowing a situation is bad, but also thinking it is rather funny   p. 46

My Personal Dictionary

My Personal Dictionary

Writing Checklist

1. I followed the directions for writing.

2. My writing shows that I read and understood the article.

3. I started each sentence with a capital letter.

4. I put a punctuation mark at the end of each sentence.

5. My sentences all have a subject and a verb.

6. I capitalized proper nouns.

7. I read my writing aloud and listened for missing words.

8. I used a dictionary to check words that don't look right.

◆ **Use the chart below to check off the things on the list that you have done.**

✓ Checklist Numbers	Lesson Numbers								
	1	2	3	4	5	6	7	8	9
1.									
2.									
3.									
4.									
5.									
6.									
7.									
8.									

Progress Check

You can take charge of your own progress. The Comprehension and Critical Thinking Progress Graph on the next page can help you. Use it to keep track of how you are doing as you work through the lessons in this book. Check the graph often with your teacher. What types of skills cause you trouble? Talk with you teacher about ways to work on these.

A sample Comprehension and Critical Thinking Progress Graph is shown below. The first three lessons have been filled in to show you how to use the graph.

Sample Comprehension and Critical Thinking Progress Graph

◆ **Directions:** Write your percentage score for each lesson in the box under the number of the lesson. Then put a small X on the line. The X goes above the number of the lesson and across from the score you earned. Chart your progress by drawing a line to connect the Xs.

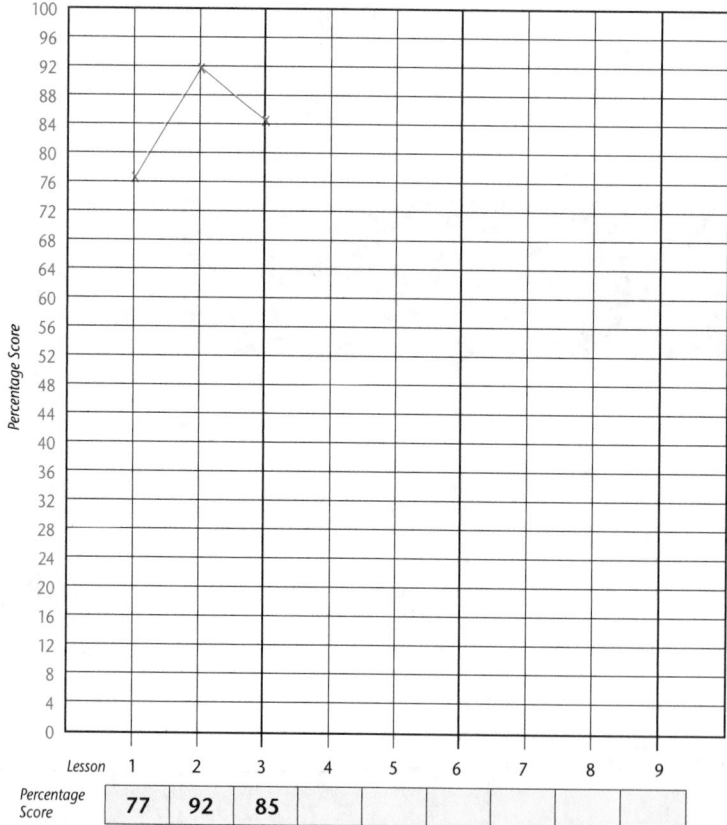

Lesson	1	2	3	4	5	6	7	8	9
Percentage Score	77	92	85						

Comprehension and Critical Thinking Progress Graph

◆ **Directions:** Write your percentage score for each lesson in the box under the number of the lesson. Then put a small X on the line. The X goes above the number of the lesson and across from the score you earned. Chart your progress by drawing a line to connect the Xs.

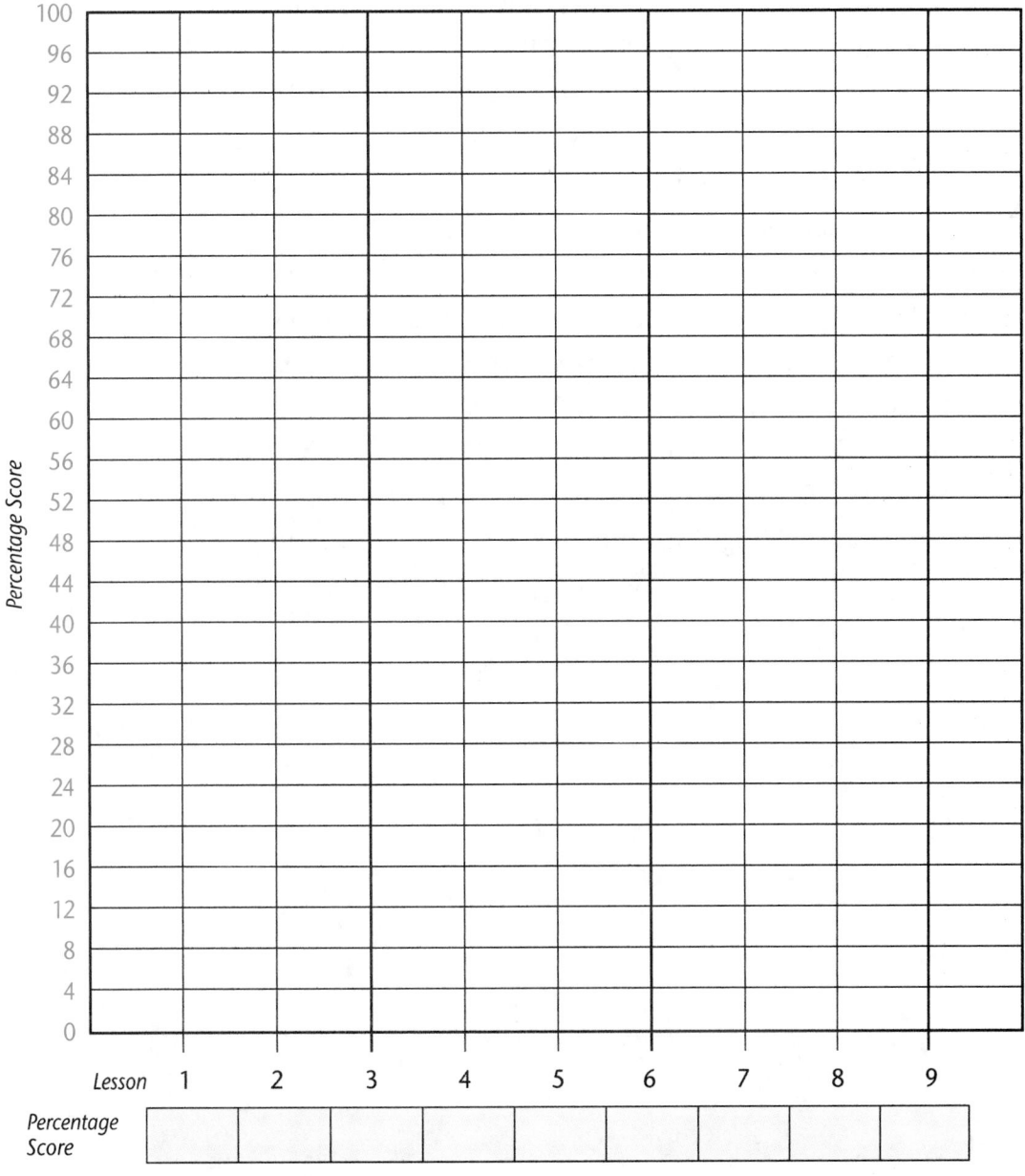

Photo Credits